SEEMS LIKE
A NICE BOY

The Story of Larry Grayson's
Rise to Stardom

SEEMS LIKE
A NICE BOY

The Story of Larry Grayson's Rise to Stardom

By Mike Malyon

Foreword by Lord Michael Grade CBE

APEX PUBLISHING LTD

First published in 2015, updated and reprinted in 2016 by
Apex Publishing Ltd
12A St. John's Road, Clacton on Sea, Essex, CO15 4BP, United Kingdom
www.apexpublishing.co.uk

British Library Cataloguing-in-Publication Data
A catalogue record for this book
is available from the British Library

ISBN 978-1-78538-473-8

Typeset in 11.5pt Baskerville Win95BT

Production Manager: Chris Cowlin
Cover Design: Hannah Blamires

Publishers Note:
The views and opinions expressed in this publication are those of the author and are not necessarily those of Apex Publishing Ltd

Copyright:
Every attempt has been made to contact the relevant copyright holders, Apex Publishing Ltd would be grateful if the appropriate people contact us on: 01255 428500 or mail@apexpublishing.co.uk

CONTENTS

DEDICATION

This book is dedicated to the memory of my mother, Joyce Malyon, who was there through all the ups and downs of Larry's life and who delighted in celebrating his eventual success.

I would like to thank my wife, Lynn, for her support and understanding as I spent time during our cruise holidays to work on this project, and my good friend, Sean Kelly, for his encouragement in getting the ball rolling.

Acknowledgements are also due to all of Larry's friends, colleagues and associates for their reminiscences which helped me to compile a personal tribute to my kind, much-missed uncle.

- Mike Malyon, October 2015

FOREWORD

I was a young agent in the late '60s helping my partner, the legendary Billy Marsh, manage Morecambe and Wise, Bruce Forsyth, Frankie Vaughan, Harry Worth, Tony Hancock and more. I built up a client list of my own and was always on the lookout for new talent.

Through my client, Leslie Crowther, I got to know Peter Dulay who was writing gags and sketches for the *Crackerjack* star. Peter rang me one day to ask me to see a comedian he had signed as manager. That was the good news. The bad news was he was appearing very late one Sunday night at the Stork Club, in London's West End — what an end to the week! But I respected Peter's judgement and trudged up west. To my surprise, the cabaret was a drag show, and Peter's discovery was given a couple of short spots to enable the 'ladies' to change costume. It didn't matter. After two minutes I knew Peter had found a rare talent.

I met Larry after the show and could see that he lived for showbiz and had taken many false dawns in his stride. I signed up as his agent the next morning and set to work. Billy and I were planning variety weeks at the Palladium and I persuaded him to give Larry a ten minute slot on a bill. I was worried ahead of opening that Larry's innuendo and double (single?) entendres might get him the wrong reputation so we carefully edited his material. He was an instant hit with the audience. They loved him, the chair, Everard Farquharson, the marrow et al. He never looked back. TV spots followed and the rest is history.

I adored Larry. His stories of variety, his generous

temperament, his surprise at his 'late' success and his appreciation marked him out as special, and I am not in the least surprised, that as the public got to know him as I did, they took him to their heart. A true original, Larry earned his place in the entertainment hall of fame the hard way. What a grey day when he left us.

- Lord Michael Grade CBE

PROLOGUE

To everyone else scurrying through the West End streets, it was a damp, dismal, grey day. But for one man, standing in a shop doorway, the weather was of no consequence. He felt he was in another world, of fantasy and delight – like being over the rainbow.

With his raincoat collar turned up, he stood there and stared across the street, his face aglow with wonder, his heart tingling with excitement. In front of him was the famous London Palladium. The showbiz Mecca; the place where the world's greatest entertainers had all appeared. And there, adorning the entrance, was a huge billboard, announcing the theatre's latest attraction, *Grayson's Scandals*, starring Larry Grayson, the newly-crowned king of camp comedy.

The man in the rust-coloured mac was transfixed. Here, in front of his very eyes, was proof that dreams really do come true. But even this was beyond his wildest expectations. From amusing his young pals in the wash-house yard, from traipsing around the working men's clubs, from years of struggle and despairing ambition… to this. Now he stood on the threshold of the ultimate achievement. The star of his own show… at the Palladium!

It was 15 October, 1974; opening night. He had already trod the Palladium stage before, in down-the-order spots, on his way up the ladder to fame, as well as being honoured with a Royal Gala appearance. But this was different. This was the big one. His photograph was twelve feet tall, above the theatre's façade. His name was in the title, up in lights. He had reached the peak of his profession.

More importantly, one very special lady was going to be out front, in the stalls, for the proudest moment of his life. She had been the closest person to him for as long as he could remember, who had become his surrogate mum, who had devoted herself to looking after him and who was now going to witness his defining triumph. That meant more to him than anything else.

And so the curtain lifted. A white Rolls Royce appeared on the stage. The door was opened by a liveried chauffeur and out stepped the star of the show... Larry Grayson. The audience erupted into raptures of applause.

Sitting among them was a straight-faced little lady, wearing a plain brown coat over a patterned dress, who wondered what all the fuss was about... Florence Hammonds.

Larry and Florence made the oddest couple; the strangest double act. He was flamboyant, out-going, eager to amuse, always happy to be the centre of attention. She was shy, inward, quiet, completely unselfish and only interested in his well-being. He was full of personality and wit, with a natural talent to make people laugh. She was totally devoid of any sense of humour and rarely showed emotion, content to remain totally detached from everything going on around her.

But here, on this glamorous night, as Larry performed on stage and Florence stared across the footlights, there was a magical connection.

This glamorous occasion, in the centre of London's neon-lit West End, was a far cry from those austere days among the old terraced cottages of Abbey Green, Nuneaton, when twenty-year-old Florence Hammonds helped seven-year-old William Sully White face his first ever audience...

CHAPTER 1
CHILDHOOD CONCERTS IN THE WASH HOUSE YARD

Florence, or Flo, as she was known, had strung up a piece of old material between the entry and the outside lavatory. Behind it she had placed an upturned tin bath. A group of children were sitting crossed-legged on the cobbled yard. They were the audience and Flo went around collecting their admission – milk bottle tops or cigarette cards. Now the concert party was ready to start.

Flo drew back the curtain and there, standing on the bath, was little William, who everyone called Billy. He began dancing, making a tapping noise on the tin. First he sang a nursery rhyme. Then he clapped his hands. That was the signal for everyone else to applaud. Flo pulled the curtain shut – and Billy left his platform, beaming from ear to ear. He just loved showing off to all his school pals.

The scruffily-dressed gang had trooped round to his house, No. 20 Stanley Crescent on Abbey Green, Nuneaton, for the special teatime treat. They were all part and parcel of a small, tight-knit community, a mile from the market town centre, with a row of shops, a pub and an infant school.

Billy was a pale, thin, sickly lad and was often kept away from school, as Flo nursed him through a succession of childhood illnesses. He had been placed into her care when Florence's mum, Alice, died of breast cancer. Billy had come into her life six years earlier, as a nine-week-old babe in arms.

He had been taken in – under somewhat mysterious, never-fully-explained circumstances – by Flo's stepfather, Jim Hammonds, a hard-working coalminer. He had married Alice after she had been widowed when her husband, James Catcliffe, was killed in action in the First World War.

Just why Jim Hammonds agreed to foster baby Billy is anyone's guess – and was never divulged. As well as Florence, he also had another stepdaughter, May, and their tiny, two-up-two-down cottage was already crowded enough. But Billy was welcomed with open arms and Alice adored him.

Whatever the reasons for the fostering arrangement – which never became a legal adoption – Jim and Alice both knew that Billy had been born illegitimately to a woman called Ethel White.

She originally came from Hook Norton, a village forty-eight miles away in another county, off the beaten path between Banbury and Oxford. She had moved to live in Hinckley and, at almost thirty- years-old, had become pregnant through an affair with a factory foreman named William Sully, who hailed from the Nuneaton area and who was either not able, or too reluctant, to continue the relationship. It seems that Ethel's condition brought about an almost immediate parting of the ways.

Ethel's family was well-to-do and she went to her sister's home in Banbury to have her baby son, who was named after his real father. After a short time in a convalescent nursing home, Ethel agreed to hand over little William into the care of the Hammonds family. It's never been revealed why she made this decision or how it came about.

Even an elderly relative of the White family, still living in Hook Norton many years later, failed to provide any answers. She told me: "As far as anyone in the village was aware, Ethel simply left to live somewhere else. There was some talk that she had become friendly with a man who had been working near our village as part of a road crew. We did hear that Ethel had had a baby boy and that he had been given away to be brought up by a family in Nuneaton."

No further details or explanation was forthcoming although, bizarrely, I was shown a hitherto unrevealed photograph of William Sully White as a baby being held by his real mother.

It seems that, not long after it was taken, Ethel travelled on the train from Banbury to Nuneaton to deliver her son into the safekeeping of Jim and Alice Hammonds.

When, six years later, Alice tragically passed away, Flo was given the responsibility of looking after Billy. It was either that or he would have to be sent away to live in a children's home – and Flo took on the task, dropping her one and only boyfriend in the process.

Ethel was an occasional visitor to the Hammonds' household and Billy initially knew her as aunty. She was a petite, neat woman, with tightly permed hair and rimless spectacles, who played the piano and led a quiet, spinster's life. After giving away her son, she moved from Hinckley to Barwell, six miles from Nuneaton across the Leicestershire border, where she worked as a housekeeper and barmaid.

Ethel apparently severed her connections with the rest of the White family back in Oxfordshire, as the shame over her illegitimate child was puritanically concealed.

Billy only discovered Ethel's true identity when he was about nine. He had accepted Flo's motherly role in his life and the revelation made no difference to how he felt. He continued to call Ethel by her name, although he did drop the aunty epithet. As he grew up, Billy was also told about his real father and, when he was in his early twenties, he had one fleeting glimpse of him.

Years later he told me what had happened: "I was walking with Flo in Bond Gate one wet afternoon and she suddenly pointed out a man crossing the road. 'That's your father,' she said. I remember he was a tall, distinguished looking gentleman, quite smartly dressed. I never saw him again but that vision stayed with me. As far as I know, he remained completely unaware of my existence."

It was an issue which always, subconsciously, played on Billy's mind. He knew that his background had, for whatever reason, been clouded in secrecy. I don't think he was ever told the full truth – and I don't think he actually asked too many questions. It was a situation he reluctantly accepted but never really came to terms with.

I doubt if Billy ever knew – or cared – about what became of William Sully. It is thought his never-to-be-known father was married with a family and lived in Leicestershire. Many years later, when Larry Grayson had become a household name, it seems that people purporting to be related to Sully did try to make contact with him. He told me: "A letter arrived out of the blue from someone claiming to be a member of my real father's family. I was not remotely interested. The letter went straight into the bin."

The link between Ethel White and the Hammonds is an intriguing one, the truth of which is never likely to be unravelled. Oxfordshire could have been a connection. That was Ethel's home county and, for some unknown reason, Alice's first husband, James Catcliffe, who originally hailed from Staffordshire before moving to Nuneaton, joined the Oxfordshire and Bucks Regiment before going off to war. He died, as a Lance Corporal on

4

the battlefields between France and Belgium in 1916, aged thirty-two. His name is inscribed on the war memorial in Nuneaton's Riversley Park – and it was always pointed out to me whenever I walked past the stone obelisk, in the company of either my uncle Bill or aunty Flo.

With regards to William Sully, it is almost certain he was related in some way or another to either James Catcliffe or his wife, Alice. Indeed, on the couple's marriage certificate, in 1906, one of the scrawled witness signatures looks suspiciously like 'William Sully'.

It is thought that William Sully worked for a time at the old Grotto Laundry in Bond Gate, Nuneaton. One theory is that he had a liaison with Ethel, while she was living in Hinckley. It's likely that he was already married and unwilling to take on the responsibility when Ethel fell pregnant. The conclusion, therefore, is that Alice, as a relative of William Sully through her first marriage, persuaded her second husband, Jim Hammonds, to accept baby Billy as their own little boy – especially as Florence and May were daughters she already had when they had wed seven years earlier.

As was often the case in those days, family indiscretions and private arrangements between relatives remained very much in the closet. They were never openly discussed and it is probable to assume that no one else, other than the three main characters involved – Alice, Jim and Ethel – ever knew the actual circumstances, so the secret died with them. I'm not sure whether Billy himself or, indeed Flo, ever learned the real truth. It's fairly certain that the rest of the family, including my mum, were also kept in the dark.

The fact that no official adoption was applied for and that there is a definite likeness – in both personality and looks – linking Billy and Flo's sister, May, only adds weight to the probability of a family connection.

How believable is it to accept that a baby from the backwoods of rural Oxfordshire was simply given away to complete strangers living in a cramped, terraced house in a Warwickshire mining town? And when you consider that those strangers were a lowly-paid pit worker and his wife who already had two daughters, the credibility becomes even more stretched.

The version, recounted as part of the Larry Grayson story many years later, was that the Hammonds had answered a newspaper advert 'home wanted for baby boy' and had collected him off a train at Nuneaton. This was the version Larry stuck to and, actually, recounted to me. But it has never been verified. No such advert has been traced – and, in any case, why would it be placed in a Nuneaton paper by someone living in an Oxfordshire village?

One thing I do recall is my great-granddad, Jim Hammonds, once mentioning to me how he had carried little Billy in his arms from the railway station to their home in Abbey Green, where Alice, Flo and May were waiting to welcome him.

Despite the hush-hush arrangement, some degree of contact was maintained between the Hammonds and the Whites. When Billy was grown up and needed some money to put down as a deposit for a house in Clifton Road, he got in touch with uncle Ralph White in Hook Norton who gave him a loan. He actually told me about this – and was proud of the fact that it was paid back religiously every week, through an account at the small Post Office on the corner of Clifton Road and Tomkinson Road. There were also occasions when Billy made the effort to visit some of the White relations in Banbury and in his will he did leave a sum of money to one of Ethel's nephews.

Whatever lay behind the reasons for his arrival, little Billy was an idolised member of the Hammonds' household and spoiled rotten. Alice would proudly push him around The Green in a second-hand pram, showing him off to the neighbours. She and Jim had a baby boy to complete their family and everyone was happy.

On Sundays, they would all go to morning service at the Abbey Church in nearby Manor Court Road and, when it was fine, would take picnics on Weddington Fields, across the babbling brook. Despite the austerity, Jim made sure there was always food on the table and coal in the grate. As Billy became a toddler, he learned his two-times table and his alphabet; he sat on his foster mum's knee and sang nursery rhymes.

Then came a bombshell when Alice was suddenly struck down with cancer. She went into hospital to have a breast removed – which was an uncommon operation in the 1920s – but never recovered properly and died on 30 March, 1930. Billy was aged just six-and-a-half. He was too young to understand what had happened. But, subconsciously, such a devastating incident struck him deeply. The pain stayed with him forever. He would say, in later years, how he had lost two mums in childhood, through no fault of his own.

Now, even at an early age, there was to be a third matriarchal woman to come into his life – his stepsister, Flo, who was handed the task of bringing him up.

At the time, she was courting her one and only boyfriend, a lad called Bert Phillips. But her dad, Jim, made it clear that, following the tragic death of Alice, Flo would have to be the new 'woman of the house'. The responsibility fell to her to do the cooking, cleaning, shopping – and the caring for Billy.

Although she had no option, Flo still unhesitatingly accepted the decision. Boyfriend Bert was told starkly that he would have to stay away, as Flo now had to devote her complete attention to caring for little Billy. There was never again room for anyone else in her life.

At the time, Flo was twenty-years-old and had a hip disability. It was a condition she had been born with, which was never medically treated and which, in later life, was to leave her almost crippled. She also struggled to read and write, which was possibly caused by dyslexia – then a largely unknown and undiagnosed affliction.

But Flo had a gentle, kind, giving nature, which stood her in good stead for the role she was landed with. My earliest memories of aunty Flo were when I went as a child with my mum on visits to Clifton Road. Flo used to religiously save the picture cards in packets of tea to give me – and they were handed over with great ceremony as soon as I walked through the door. I can also still distinctly recall the bristle of my great-granddad Jim's moustache when I was told to kiss him on the cheek.

Not long after Alice's death, Flo's elder sister, May – who was to become my grandma – had left home to be married to Charlie Roberts and live in Coventry. Back in Nuneaton, Jim Hammonds worked long shift hours at Haunchwood Colliery while young Billy was already getting to be quite a handful. Apart from a string of illnesses – "I'd catch everything that was going, twice sometimes," – he was also demanding lots of attention.

He was enrolled at the nearby Abbey Infants School where, he was to discover more than fifty years later, that his birth certificate surname Sully White was written alongside his school name William Hammonds.

The question of his identity and the confusion of having a number of different names was a constant issue. He once remarked to me: "No wonder, I felt so mixed up. I never really knew who I was. I went from William Sully White to William White, then Billy Hammonds, then Billy Breen, then Larry Grayson."

As a youngster, he would be taken by Flo, hand-in-hand, to school every day. He would be dressed in grey shorts, a plain shirt, striped woollen tie and V-necked jumper. His shoes would always be spotless – a habit he never grew out of. He and Flo would hurry the short distance to the school gates, as the bell sounded. Any pupils not getting into their classroom by the time it stopped, were marked down as late and would be in trouble. Often Flo would turn up in the playground on her own, with a sick note for Billy, who had been left at home in bed, with a cold, a fever, measles or suchlike.

Billy admitted that he never enjoyed school very much, but he still kept fond memories of the teachers, such as Miss Mayo, who would choose pupils to have the honour of ringing the morning bell, and Miss Booth, who he met again many years later during the making of a television documentary to mark his sixtieth birthday. "She was a little nervous that I would not remember her," he said. "But how could I forget? I can even remember her telling our class that she was getting married."

There was another teacher, Miss Alderson, who used to stand on a chair and conduct the school choir with her eyes closed "which always fascinated me." Billy once got into trouble for pushing a little girl called Amy Proctor into some pig swill and also found himself being picked on by one of the school bullies. "The teachers had put up a notice in the playground about spitting and I accidentally dropped a gobstopper from my mouth," he recalled. "This lad saw me and threatened to say to the teachers that I'd spat it out if I didn't give him my sweets. It was nothing less than blackmail and he kept it up for weeks."

When he revisited his school, for his sixtieth birthday TV documentary, he was amazed to be shown the original register. Looking at the list of names, he remarked: "Ooh, look, William Starkey. And there's Dorothy Cartwright. She was very clever."

He recalled how fellow pupils were forever being bossily roped in to make up an audience or accompany him on the makeshift stage for his backyard concerts. "You can be my ugly sisters," he would tell some of the girls, while others were ordered to "sit still and listen." They only agreed to be involved on the promise of being served warmed-up stale cakes afterwards. When it came to his performance, Billy was keen to do things properly and would go around the neighbours, begging bits of material to make up a costume.

There were two events at Abbey Green School that brought untold pleasure to Billy: The Christmas nativity and the Maypole dance. When the teachers were deciding on the parts for the nativity play, Billy quickly volunteered to be one of the Wise Men. He had set his sights on the gold and glitter outfits to be worn by the Three Kings – there was no way he was being put into sackcloth as one of the shepherds. Even at such an early age, glamour beckoned.

He also had the time of his life when the school celebrated May Day, making sure he was given one of the brightly coloured ribbons to skip around the maypole. He called it "real joy."

For the benefit of the TV documentary, the maypole dance was specially recreated in that same playground, Larry's eyes lit up as he watched the young pupils twirling around, going in and out – and he couldn't resist the urge to join in, chuckling as he took his turn. It made a lovely, unrehearsed sequence for the cameras.

Looking back to his childhood days, Larry also vividly remembered seeing his first-ever live show. "It was *Babes in the Wood* at the old Nuneaton Hippodrome. I was about four but I was fascinated by the sight of the make-up worn by the cast, their brown faces and blue eye shadow," he said. "I thought 'that's for me' and I started to tell everyone at school that I was going to be on the stage when I grew up. The other boys imagined driving steam trains or racing motor cars and would run around making various engine noises, like 'sh,sh,sh and br,br,br'. I was more interested in watching the girls playing with their dollies."

It soon began to dawn on young Billy that he was not like the other boys. Gradually, something inside made him feel different. He was not the least bit bothered about joining their rough-and-tumble activities. There was no fun for him in kicking a ball about, playing tig or collecting conkers. Instead, he would rather stand in the corner of the playground, where the girls congregated, and whose giggling games seemed more of an attraction. He realised he never really fitted in and years later, would describe himself as "a living, breathing mistake."

It used to amuse him, after he had become famous, to hear people announce they had been to school with him and insist that he had been one of their footballing chums. He said: "Can you imagine, me playing football? I don't think I've ever kicked a football in my life – or ever wanted to. It's funny, really, because from the number of people who love to claim they sat by me at school, we would have needed to have had a class of about 200!"

Looking back, he also realised how those school days had helped shape his destiny. He found it was easier to be popular by being amusing, rather than by having to prove himself among his more macho peers. He quickly learned the lesson of how to be accepted by both sexes, without particularly identifying with either – which may explain the enigma of his own actual sexuality in later years.

Away from school, Billy soaked up life in Stanley Crescent, which held nostalgic memories. He told me: "It was such a lovely atmosphere, even though the conditions were pretty basic. There was a tap in the back yard for the whole row of houses to use. Friday nights would be bath time when everyone was rushing around, filling and boiling kettles. Dad would come home, caked in grime from the pit, and sit in a tin bath in front of a raging fire, which Flo had already got ready. Then we would sit around this big square table to have our tea, often home-cooked chips and sometimes a steaming hot stew, with thick slices of bread and butter. After Flo had cleared away the plates, Dad would sit in his armchair and light up his pipe and we'd listen to music on the wireless. Oh, what happy days."

Billy left Abbey Green Infants at the age of eleven and moved onto Manor Park, which had opened in 1928 as the town's new secondary school. Charles Bates was the headmaster – and Billy soon made his mark, although not academically. After being ticked off for impersonating Katharine Hepburn in class, he also put his hand up to take part in the school concert. A teacher asked what he would do and Billy immediately replied: "I'll do my Eddie Cantor act." He then went straight into it, singing every line of two songs, 'If You Knew Susie' and 'Ma, He's Making Eyes At Me'. It was a startling, impromptu performance. The teacher cowered against the blackboard, completely taken aback by this cocky little character – while the rest of the class sat in stunned silence, with their mouths gaping wide.

Billy had picked up on Hepburn and Cantor from his love of the cinema. It had been a weekly treat from Flo to be taken to the pictures – the Palace in Queen's Road, the Scala in Abbey Street, the Royal in Stratford Street or, occasionally, the Grand at Chapel End. On very special occasions, Billy and Flo would sit 'in the Gods' at the imposing Prince of Wales Theatre in Bond Gate, to watch live variety shows. There was even a rare trip on the bus to Coventry to see the stars of the day perform at the city centre Hippodrome. Thanks entirely to Flo, he became enthralled and absorbed in the world of films and shows.

He used to talk about the time Nuneaton's new cinema opened, the luxurious ABC Ritz at the top of Abbey Street. It had plush red velvet seats, a carpeted, mirrored foyer and a uniformed doorman. When Judy Garland's *Easter Parade* showed there, Billy went three nights in a row and even took a photograph, showing the placards outside, which he kept in a scrapbook. Billy lived for such outings and the sheer thrill of sitting in a darkened cinema or hushed theatre to be entertained from the screen or stage never left him.

One of those early artists who created an impression on him was Arthur Lucan. He performed as Old Mother Riley and Billy went with Flo to the Coventry Hippodrome, paying six old pence to sit in the upper circle and watch the 1940s' comedy film star in action, complete in long skirt, a shawl, a tatty grey wig, a bonnet and boots. Lucan appeared alongside his wife, Kitty McShane, who played his flame-haired daughter. As a youngster, Billy had watched several of the Old Mother Riley films at the pictures and he was excited to see this eccentric-looking character live on stage.

Almost forty years later, when he was appearing in Hull, Billy found the final resting place of Lucan, whose real name was Arthur Towle and who had died in a dressing

13

room at the city's Tivoli Theatre in 1954. Shocked to find the grave overgrown with grass and weeds, he spent some time tidying it up himself. The local newspaper reported the fact, which led to local fans rallying around to renovate the area around the burial plot and clean the headstone.

CHAPTER 2
LURE OF SHOWBIZ WITH
THE VARY LITES

Without any qualifications, Billy left school aged fourteen. The family home had, meanwhile, moved to Priory Street in Stockingford and – as a twist of fate that would change his life forever – it was through becoming friendly with the people living next door that Billy took his first steps on the entertainment ladder.

Alf Freeman was the local butcher, who also sang around the local clubs with his wife, Nell, daughter, Freda, and her boyfriend, George Smith. They were billed as a concert party and called themselves The Vary Lites. Billy was immediately taken up with his new, out-of-the-ordinary neighbours and was constantly making a bee-line into their house to watch rehearsals around the parlour piano. It wasn't long before Billy was itching to join in, declaring that it was his ambition to go on the stage.

Alf asked him: "Can you sing?"

Billy replied, "No."

Can you dance?"

"No."

"Can you play a musical instrument?"

Billy again said, "No."

"Well, that's a good start," said Alf, "so I suppose you will just have to be yourself."

Freda, who had a beautiful voice, gave Billy some singing lessons. "He spent hours at the piano with me but it was a struggle," she recalled many years later. "He just couldn't reach the notes. But we tried out one song, which he could virtually talk his way through and after three weeks of practice, it did not sound too bad." That song was a risqué, music hall offering 'In the Bushes at the Bottom of the Garden' and, after much pestering, Alf consented to let Billy perform it during The Vary Lites' next outing.

The booking was for a wedding reception at Fife Street Working Men's Club. Billy was fourteen. He was dressed by Nell in a piped jacket, white trousers and straw boater. Midway through the group's act, he was introduced, as Billy Hammonds, and performed his ditty. It ended with the line 'And the old tom cat took the tabby next door... to the bushes at the bottom of the garden'. Billy left the stage to polite applause – and was instantly hooked. He was paid five shillings, his first ever wage, which clinched his decision to make this his career.

"I had already had one job, at a shoe shop, which I hated. I only stayed two days," he explained. "I also did a stint as a knocker-up, going round to miners' houses and tapping on their bedroom windows with a long pole, to wake them for their early morning shifts. Let's face it, that job was never going to lead to a career and didn't last long. In any case, the going wage then for shop work was only ten bob for a full six-day week. I suddenly started getting that by going on stage just two nights a week with Alf and Nell. I just loved it. I was in my element – and never earned another penny from doing anything else, ever again."

Alf and Nell were real characters, very theatrical, and told their story when their young protégé was the subject of *This Is Your Life* in December 1972. When Eamonn Andrews asked Alf what Billy did during his act in those days, he replied: "The same as he does now – he just messed about."

For the boy comedian it was a swift learning curve. But he lapped it up, doing the rounds of the local clubs and gradually building up his repertoire, with Nell offering encouragement – in between secret sips of gin from a china cup, so that Alf wouldn't notice. Her husband, meanwhile, was the driving force behind the group and insisted that each of them looked presentable on stage and treated the audience with respect. He was a stickler for punctuality and wouldn't dream of using any material that might offend. All these tips were taken firmly on board by Billy – and remained with him throughout his career.

One of the regular dates for The Vary Lites was at Attleborough Labour Club, which just so happened to be right opposite Everard Road. That was a sheer coincidence and was not where Billy got the name for one of his famous characters. As he said on *This Is Your Life*: "That came from the time I was in digs in Bradford. I had arrived on the Sunday night and the landlady offered me a cup of tea and a fairy cake – that's where I got that from! Anyway, this lad then came through the door bouncing a football. The landlady called from the kitchen: "Is that you, Everard?" He was about eleven and I thought, "He's going to bless you when he's eighteen."

It was during one concert at the Labour Club that Billy got his first taste of an unreceptive audience. "He got the bird," recalled Alf. "I don't know whether it was his singing or the song. He came off the stage quite upset and I thought his career may have finished that night."

But, thanks to Alf and Nell's persuasion, Billy carried on and gradually began to introduce more bits of humorous banter into his act. Back in Priory Street, the women neighbours were always in and out of each other's houses and Billy would sit in the corner, listening to all their chit-chat. He lapped it up; the way they talked about their ailments, how they gossiped about one another, all their subtle, female nuances. Subconsciously, it was material being stored away at the back of his mind, which would come in so useful as he went on to develop his trademark style.

Not far from Priory Street was a house once lived in by Polly Button, who had been murdered in a notorious case in 1832. Her boyfriend, Joe Danks, was found guilty and publicly hanged in Warwick. Billy used to pretend he had seen Polly Button's ghost and would make up stories about the building being haunted – much to the amusement, if not belief, of whoever was listening.

As the Second World War approached, the Hammonds moved again to live in Harefield Road, opposite a waste piece of ground where Nuneaton Bus Station now stands and near the town's old cattle market. The family home became a refuge for a flock of friendly American soldiers, who were stationed in Nuneaton, awaiting orders to join the D-Day invasion. They loved spending off-duty hours in the company of their English hosts and would call into Harefield Road, where Flo would serve them a typical English tea – fish and chips, or sausage and mash – while Billy relished the opportunity to show off to this new audience.

The GIs found themselves being entertained by someone the like of which they had never come across before. Billy's wit and his comically-off-beat demeanour were like a breath of fresh air in the otherwise claustrophobic atmosphere of war-torn Britain.

Joyce Roberts, the daughter of Flo's sister, May, would regularly travel over from blitz-hit Coventry to stay with the Hammonds. She said: "The house was always full of people and laughter. It was great. The Yanks looked very dashing, had lovely manners and used to bring Flo and

Billy gifts of chewing gum and tins of fruit. They loved being made welcome. They used to call it their little English home."

Joyce – my mum – was six years younger than Billy. They bonded like brother and sister, which is how they labelled themselves to anyone who asked. "We always had so much fun. A fairground used to visit the land opposite the Harefield Road house and we would sit looking out of the window watching the crowds flocking around and the rides, all brightly lit up. I remember one night we spotted that a woman had dropped a box of chocolates and Bill made me run down to the street and pick it up. We then ate the whole lot in one go," said Joyce.

"Bill would lead Flo a merry dance and was always tantalising her and playing tricks. Once he tied her up to a chair and then went upstairs and began waving this model of a woman's leg out of the window, startling the passers-by. I don't know where he got the prop from, I think it was from a shop display but I remember Flo going mad from the kitchen, saying 'I'll smack your legs.' Of course, all these antics were going on while my granddad Jim was either at work or out working as a voluntary fire warden, keeping an eye out for bombs and incendiaries."

It was on the night of 17 May, 1941 that Jim's alertness saved his family from almost certain death. Billy explained: "When the air raid siren sounded, we usually sheltered under the stairs. This particular night, Nell was stopping with us and joined me and Flo in the cupboard. But my father came in and said the raid looked like it was going to be a bad one and told us to go down the underground shelter nearby. We did what he suggested and about an hour later we heard this massive explosion. When we eventually came out of the shelter, our house was nowhere to be seen. It had been completely floored."

Billy, Flo and Jim were left with just the clothes they stood up in. But they were not alone. That night, the German bombers destroyed 380 houses in Nuneaton, with 10,000 being damaged altogether – and 110 people were killed. A stonemason's, opposite the Hammonds house, also took a direct hit and a headstone cross, bearing the inscription 'Peace' was the only thing left standing.

Queues formed at the Town Hall where items of clothing were handed out. Forms were also distributed offering the homeless temporary accommodation. The Hammonds were billeted in a house in Ansley, which was virtually derelict, with holes in the ceiling and freezing cold. They also spent some time lodging with the Freemans back in Priory Street, as The Vary Lights continued touring the clubs and also entertaining the troops stationed at the nearby Bramcote Barracks.

The group's protégé was happy to keep collecting his ten bob (50p) a week and by now was being introduced as 'Billy Breen', saying he had chosen the stage name because 'it sounded clean'. One day the call-up papers for National Service dropped through the letterbox and Billy had to go to the Sibree Hall in Coventry for the required medical.

As he walked into the room, mincing theatrically as if he was making a stage entrance, Billy was met by a stern-faced orderly who took one look at him and said: "Oh, no, the war's not that bad!" Probably because of his pasty pallor – and even maybe due to the fact that he had not completely wiped away the stage make-up from the previous night's concert party – Billy was marked down as a grade four, which made him exempt for National Service, but also excluded him from joining ENSA – the forces' entertainment regiment, which is what he'd set his sights on.

Billy was never given any official reason why he failed

the military medical. It was not until he had his first serious illness, many years later, that he discovered in his notes a record of having an irregular heartbeat. "That was certainly news to me. I never had a problem with my heart. What a shame – the army never knew what they missed."

Instead of going abroad to amuse the troops near the front line – an exercise which launched the careers of many up-and-coming comedians – Billy stayed in Nuneaton and performed on shows organised in Riversley Park. These *Holidays at Home* events were designed to keep people's minds off the war and featured various local artists. Billy hooked up with two singers; Ken Daniels and Hazel Cook. For a while he formed a double act with Ken and began dressing in drag, for a spot as a female impersonator.

"Billy was quite poor and only had one pair of trousers. When I called round for him, he would usually be standing at the ironing board in his underpants, pressing his trousers," recalled Ken. "Whenever he got a few bob together, he would spend it on a new frock. That part of his act used to cause quite a stir because it was a novelty in those days to see a man dressed up as a woman. His local popularity really began to take off."

As the war came to an end, the Hammonds moved into a terrace house at No. 52 Clifton Road – where they would remain for almost thirty years. Jim was still working at the pit and Flo was also earning, with a job serving meals and clearing tables in the canteen at the Courtaulds factory in Marlborough Road.

Billy decided to branch out and joined a new concert party, labelled *Tomorrow's Stars* and produced by a former music hall entertainer Harry Leslie. It was 1947 and their tour of Devon happened to coincide with one of the harshest winters ever to hit Britain. They played village halls, often in the middle of nowhere, and slept on church floors and in cars, eating sausages cooked in tin lids.

Once, because of a power failure, the audience had to go home and fetch oil lamps so the show could continue. It was as bleak as it could get and one night Billy was trapped by a snow drift in the back of a car, with his eyelids frozen together. Harry Leslie got him out and said: "Don't worry, when we get you in that hall, with a log fire burning and with you in your cape and that woman's bonnet, you'll soon be all right."

When, in later years, Billy looked back on that tour he said: "We played at some tiny, isolated villages in parish and church halls but we were made very welcome. Everyone in the community turned out to watch the show and I don't think any one of them had seen a female impersonator before. There were eight of us and we did little sketches, songs and dances, with a few jokes thrown in. It was wonderful training. Mr Leslie used to put us through rehearsals and we were taught how to walk on and walk off and how to stand properly. But the main memory is how cold it was. We used to warm ourselves up in the local pub. Half a bitter was three old pence. My wages were £2 a week."

Billy returned to Nuneaton, where he palled up with a self-taught but brilliant pianist, Ronnie Hollis. The pair could often be found socialising in the back room of the Nag's Head or the Holly Bush in Bond Gate, where Billy would hold court, with Ronnie as his laconic straight man. Ronnie would regularly get work as the accompanist for the Friday and Saturday night and Sunday lunchtime concerts around the local clubs and pubs and was more often than not the butt of Billy's humour during his act – which Ronnie took with a pinch of salt and a deadpan expression.

Billy used to get bookings all over the Midlands and it was at a club in Swadlincote, in Derbyshire, that he was seen by Leicester-based theatrical agent, Barry Wood. He was putting a cast together for the 1950 summer season in Redcar, on the north east coast, and offered Billy four months solid work, at a wage of £15 a week.

The variety show, staged at The Pier Pavilion, was titled *Radio Tymes*, with twice nightly performances at 6.00 p.m. and 8.00 p.m. and a backdrop loaned by the BBC. Billy was given his own second half spot, appearing in drag in a routine called 'A Pretty Girl is Like a Melody'. He also appeared in various skits and musical numbers with other members of the company, which included Vic Ray and Lucille ('dance stylists') Syd Cheshire ('The Lad from Yorkshire'), ventriloquist Winston Foxwell, Billy Windsor, Charlie Bruce, Doris Colledge and a double act from Leicester, Gary Grande and David Mars, who struck up a lifetime friendship with the comic from Nuneaton. In the two penny programme for the show, Billy Breen was tagged 'Oh Boy! What a Girl!' and 'The Breezy Baron of Burlesque'.

The *Radio Tymes* production was voted a huge success, not only by the regular Redcar theatre-goers and holidaymakers but also by people from the surrounding towns and villages. So much so, that Barry Wood was asked to bring back similar shows for the next two summers, which Billy also appeared in. He thoroughly enjoyed those seaside days and forever afterwards had a soft spot for Redcar. In fact, in his will he left £10,000 for the local lifeboat station, "to repay some of the kindness shown all those years ago by the townsfolk."

In between the summer engagements, Barry Wood also found other work for Billy at theatres around the country. In one of them, the top of the bill was legendary comic Jimmy James. One night he called Billy into his dressing room and said: "I've been watching your act. You've got it, son. You will be a star one day."

While Wood acted as his agent – on the other end of a phone line – Billy managed himself as far as local bookings went. But in 1955 he received a call, following a small write-up in *The Stage* newspaper, to perform at the Nuffield Centre, in London, which was a venue for servicemen but also served as a talent-spotting showcase.

In the audience this particular night happened to be one of the capital's most influential agents, Evelyn Taylor. At the end of the night she went backstage and gave Billy her card. "Come and see me in my office tomorrow," she said. The result of that meeting provided Billy with his first big break.

CHAPTER 3
FIRST BIG BREAK ON THE
VARIETY THEATRE CIRCUIT

Evelyn Taylor was steeped in the business and had once been a leading lady with one of Billy's heroes, the late, great, Birmingham-born comedian Sid Field. When Billy duly turned up at her Chandos Street office in the West End the next day, she was gushing with praise. "You've got Sid's warmth and you've got marvellous timing – impeccable. We're going to put you out in variety but we've got to find you a new name, get you some new clothes and have some professional photographs taken."

The first task was the name. Eve's secretary, Nina Haycock, was also in the room and said she had walked past the Empire that morning and noticed the musical starring Kathryn Grayson.

"What about Grayson?" she suggested.

Eve looked up. "Yes I like that. Now what can we get to go with it. Tommy? Bobby? Freddy? Larry? Yes, Larry. Write it down. Yes, Larry Grayson. I like it. Do you like it, Billy? That's it then. From now on you are Larry Grayson."

Eve immediately picked up the phone and called top booking agent, Joe Collins – whose daughter, Joan, was later to become a big Hollywood star.

"Hello Joe," said Eve. "You know that boy I told you about from the Nuffield last night? Well, he's here now. Larry Grayson. I'll send him round."

Minutes later, Eve's latest discovery was in front of the

much-respected Mr Collins, who said he had heard 'lots of nice things' about him and that he could immediately offer Larry four dates – opening the following week at the Hippodrome, Dudley, and going on to the Regal, Great Yarmouth, with Dot Squires and then at Hastings with Ann Shelton before appearing at the Parade in Skegness, on the Carole Levis bill.

As his first official manager, Eve Taylor began to pull all the strings. Along with a change of name, she decided that the act had to be focused on camp comedy, which meant an end to dressing up as a female impersonator. Larry Grayson was now being heralded as 'the new Sid Field', after the Birmingham-born comic who had become a West End star but died in 1950, aged forty-six, from a heart attack.

Larry never copied Field but there was a similarity between their style of humour; the sideways glance, the raised eyebrows, the knowing winks. Larry came up with a novel, non-Field idea of using a bentwood chair as a prop to lean on. "Let's just have a change of scenery," he would say, as he moved the chair from the right side to the left. This little gimmick, together with his nudge-nudge, down-to-earth, amusing, story-telling act, attracted a lot of attention and Larry was soon travelling all over the country, at the 'No. 1' theatres, including the renowned Moss Empire circuit.

It was definitely a step up the ladder; an exciting time, mixing and performing with some of the top variety artists of the era at some of the leading venues. But it could also be a grim, lonely existence, living out of a suitcase, trooping around from town to town by train and searching out and stopping in theatrical digs. It meant always travelling on a Sunday, to arrive at the theatre for Monday morning band-call. More often than not, groups of acts, costumes and props in hand, would meet up on Crewe railway station, swopping tales of rotten audiences, draughty dressing rooms and dodgy landladies.

"We would all gather on the platform, waiting for our respective trains," he recalled. "It would be: 'Where were you last week? Ooh, not Bradford. I had a terrible time there. Now where you off to? Aah, Leicester. You'll do okay – don't forget to call in at Mrs Randle's and tell her I sent you. If you're lucky she'll have something warm waiting for you...' Being in variety in those days was like being part of another world. Artists would be permanently on the move all over the country. We'd be bumping into each other on railway platforms, as we made our way to and from engagements."

There were many occasions when Larry would be in some cold, bleak digs after returning from the theatre and feel terribly alone. He told me how he would lie on his bed in a tiny attic room, stare up at the peeling wallpaper on the ceiling and wonder what it was all about. Where was it all leading? Would he ever, one day, make it?

As it was, Larry held onto his dreams and ploughed ahead. Even as a down-the-bill performer, the money was not bad – £16 for eight performances. It meant that after paying his board and lodging and travelling expenses, he could still send £3 every week to help Flo and Jim back home in Nuneaton.

Touring in variety, week in week out, also provided invaluable experience. Working alongside stalwarts of the stage, the seasoned pros, was the best form of apprenticeship he could ever get. Larry soaked it up, listened, learned and kept his hopes alive that one day he would finally be up there alongside the best of them, with his name four inches tall headlining the posters, instead of being so low down it almost fell off the bottom.

With time on his hands in strange towns, waiting for the evening show to begin, Larry had the opportunity to while away endless hours enjoying his favourite pastime – going to the pictures. 'Theatricals' usually got free admission during the day and Larry would do the rounds of all the cinemas in the vicinity – sometimes more than once. When he was appearing in Scunthorpe, he went every afternoon to see Deanna Durbin in *Something in the Wind*. It would be the same if a film was on starring his beloved Judy Garland – he would be there in the cinema stalls for each daytime screening, with his eyes glued to the screen, lip-syncing every word.

His adulation for Judy began when Flo took him to the Palace Cinema in Nuneaton to watch the young Hollywood singer in *The Pigskin Parade*. He said: "The first glimpse did it for me. It was love at first sight. There was something about Judy which just clicked in my heart. She was such a sweet girl, who could act anyone's socks off and had a magnificent voice. From the very moment I first clapped eyes on her, there was no one else. I used to live for the release of her next film and collected every one of her records."

As a staunch Garland fan, Billy twice watched her perform live, in concerts at De Montfort Hall, Leicester, and at the Dominion Theatre in London. Then, on 29 November, 1964, he actually came face to face with his idol. He was a card-carrying member of her International Fan Club and it had been arranged for Judy to attend a group meeting at the Russell Hotel in London. Billy travelled down with his friend and fellow Garland devotee, Reg Needle, from Leicester.

"We were both an absolute bag of nerves," he recalled. "For one thing, we never thought for a moment that Judy would turn up. Reg said she was bound to let us down.

"But then the door opened and there she was; this tiny figure wrapped in a fur coat, with her hair short and with that little-girl-lost look on her face. I was in a state of shock. I could not move.

"She walked in, smiling and saying 'Hello everyone. It's so nice to meet you all.' Someone handed me her coat to hang up but I just stood there, rooted to the spot, transfixed by the sight of this woman who I had admired and loved for so many years. I just could not believe that little Dorothy from Kansas was here, in person, right in front of me. She settled down on a big chair as we all gathered around her to watch the film *The Harvey Girls*.

"She remarked 'My hair is so red in this' but I never looked at the screen – I could not take my eyes off her. In no time at all, the meeting came to an end and Judy got up to leave. I remember my friend, Reg, confronting her and giving her a lecture, telling her to make sure she looked after herself. She listened, with those huge eyes wide open, and then she gave a little wave and walked out the room. It was one of the most memorable moments of my life."

That meeting was during one of Judy's regular trips to London. She came back again in 1969 to appear at the Talk of the Town, a nightclub in Leicester Square. When the booking was announced, my uncle phoned me and said: "I'll take you to see her. I'll order some tickets." But the first reviews were unkind. Judy was thin and drawn, through illness, and was not in good form. "I'm sorry, Michael," he said. "There is no way I want you to see my Judy like that. We're not going." During the engagement Judy got married for a fourth time, to Mickey Deans, and days later she was found dead on the bathroom floor of a rented flat in Kensington, aged just forty-seven.

My uncle was devastated. *The Evening Tribune* carried a

story about the local entertainer's sadness and included a photograph showing him sitting on his front-room carpet surrounded by Judy Garland album covers. A short while later, he bought me the record of that farewell performance by Judy at the Talk of the Town. "She sounds terrible. Listen to it just the once and you will realise why it's a good job we never went to see her," he said. I still have that record, in its golden-coloured sleeve – and it has only ever been played a handful of times.

Sometime earlier, he had also given me a copy of another Judy LP – the four-sided live recording from Carnegie Hall, on 23 April, 1961, which had been hailed as 'the greatest night in show business'. It was Judy at her absolute best and, even today, gives me a thrill to listen to.

During his days in variety, the up-and-coming Larry Grayson would cross paths with many other artists, who went on to become lifelong friends. They included Tommy Austen, Tommy Packham, fellow Nuneatonian Alan Fenn and a song-and-dance double act, Barry Anthony and Ray Young.

"When I first met Larry we got chatting and he asked me who my favourite film stars were," said Barry, "I replied Judy Garland, Fred Astaire, Mickey Rooney, Rita Hayworth. What I didn't realise was that I had hit the bullseye by mentioning Judy. After that we became real genuine friends. Whenever we were around the Midlands and Billy was not working, me and Ray would head straight to Clifton Road.

"Flo would make us so welcome, with tea and sandwiches and we would sit listening to Judy records in the front room, on this big old gramophone cabinet. Flo was a treasure. She was slightly lame and I remember how she used to limp into the house, after finishing work, sometimes drenched from walking home in the rain. We would be sitting there, with the music blaring out, and Larry would immediately say 'Come on Flo, get the kettle on.' She would go straight into the kitchen and then Larry would shout: 'How about some nice fish and chips?' Without hesitation, Flo would put her coat back on and go off to the chip shop. She was a terrific woman and never batted an eyelid about anything Larry wanted."

Another friendship created on the circuit was with a former female impersonator, George Ellisia, who lived in Leamington Spa with a military gentleman called Cecil. George had been in the business for many years, since well before the war, and was quick to spot Larry's potential. He told him: "You were made to be a star. You have the timing, the quality and the warmth and you will get there one day, you'll see."

Fortunately, even though he was then quite ill and Cecil had passed away, George lived to see Larry hit the big time. The last occasion they met was when Larry visited George in a nursing home in Warwick, when the old pro looked up and smiled: "Well done. You've made me so proud."

As Larry travelled around the country, returning to Nuneaton only occasionally, Flo enjoyed the friendship of neighbours in the terraced row at Clifton Road, who would nip round most days for a cup of tea and a chat. It was a contented life for Flo and she had her dad, Jim, there to keep her company – and also to read out the weekly letters from Larry, which contained titbits of news, along with some housekeeping money.

It goes without saying that Flo was forever worrying about 'our Bill' and how he was coping. She knew he was away working but could never really comprehend the sort of business he was involved in. He was going to places she had never heard of and mixing with people who might as well have come from another planet. It was all completely above Flo's head.

Larry, meanwhile, was busy earning a living, while trying to make a showbiz name for himself. As the swinging sixties began, he also experienced the beginnings of the pop music explosion, being booked on a nationwide tour with Adam Faith, the lad from East Acton, who had hit the top of the charts with 'What Do You Want' and 'Poor Me'. Larry had the task of performing his own act – in between endless screams from an audience full of teenage girls – before finally introducing the star of the show.

This was 1960 and in the same year Larry caused a bit of a stir back in his hometown by announcing his engagement to a girl he had met during the tour.

Mary Mudd was the female vocalist in The Mudlarks, a trio made up of her and her two brothers Jeff and Fred. She and Larry became very close, very quickly, and a newspaper story in the *Nuneaton Evening Tribune* revealed their romance. Rings were exchanged – but almost as soon as it started, the relationship came to an end.

This was an episode in his life that was never again mentioned. In all the numerous interviews after he became famous, Larry chose to keep this romantic interlude a closely-guarded secret. It had come as a big surprise to his family and friends because Larry had never so much as hinted that he wanted to settle down. What on earth Flo and dad Jim ever thought can only be imagined. They met Mary once, when Larry took her to Sunday afternoon tea at Clifton Road. But the matter of any forthcoming marriage was soon dismissed. As far as anyone knows, Larry and Mary never saw each other again.

The Mudlarks had two big hits 'Lollipop' and 'Book of Love' and Mary, who was sixteen years younger than

Larry, went on to marry David Lane, who had replaced her brother, Jeff, in the group and who died from cancer in 2010.

With romantic intentions put firmly on the back-burner, rising comic Larry Grayson began to concentrate on developing and perfecting his act. He didn't do gags; he shunned the easy option of one-line jokes. Instead, he chose an appealing, almost unique, style which involved a routine of quirky, slightly-titillating, highly amusing stories about a string of make-believe friends, such as Everard, Slack Alice and Apricot Lil.

"Every neighbourhood had someone like Slack Alice," he explained. "You know, the one who always had coal no matter how short the supply was. People used to see her in the Cock and Trumpet, wearing her red hat and drinking with the coalman. It was easy to guess how Alice always happened to be so well off for slack!

"Apricot Lil came about when a woman was telling me about her friend who worked at the local jam factory. 'You know, Lil,' she'd say. 'The one who owes money to all the club books.' I couldn't place who she meant. 'Of course you know her,' my friend replied. 'Her on the apricot line. Lil in apricots.' After that Apricot Lil became a legend."

Life in variety began to get difficult for Larry in the early 1960s, as television grew to be the major entertainment medium. Theatres up and down the country felt the effect and started to struggle to survive.

"I was playing all the big dates, Birmingham, Newcastle, Leeds, Finsbury Park, Bristol – the lot. I was doing very well but as I was going round, the theatres were closing behind me. I did Leicester Palace and the next week it closed. The same happened at Derby Hippodrome – I was there the week before it went out of business."

One offer that did come Larry's way was to be an

understudy for Frankie Howerd, who was starring in a hit show in the West End, *A Funny Thing Happened on the Way to the Forum*. It was set in ancient Rome and was a precursor to a successful television programme and subsequent film that Frankie developed along the same lines a few years later, called *Up Pompeii*. Larry's style had been labelled 'Howerd-esque' because of the way that both comics made asides to the audience and complained about their surroundings. Larry never liked the comparison and immediately turned down the understudy role. He was either going to make it his way or not at all – and certainly not in someone else's shadow.

But the variety work began to dry up. There were less and less bookings to be found in the diminishing number of theatres so Larry decided to return to his roots and go back to making a living on the bread-and-butter Midlands club circuit.

He terminated his agreement with manager Evelyn Taylor and reinvented himself as Billy Breen, getting his frocks out of mothballs and resurrecting his old club act; drag in the first half then into a suit for part two. It meant turning his back on touring, shelving plans to be a star and accepting the role of being 'a big fish in a little pond'.

CHAPTER 4
BACK IN CLUBLAND -
DOING DRAG

But Billy Breen was soon one of the most popular 'turns' in clubland, being offered £5 a show and doing three or four engagements a week. He had never learned to drive and getting to dates always meant either catching a bus or train or hitching a lift with a fellow performer. He would often arrange to share the bill with Bryn Waters, a young electrician by trade and part-time singer, who lived nearby and had his own car. Bryn would pull up outside 52 Clifton Road, hoot the horn and Billy would trundle out, suitcase in hand.

The mid-60s was a heyday of club entertainment and Billy worked all the big venues in the Midlands, the working men's, social and factory clubs, which would be packed at weekends. He became a top draw and when he headed the bill in Saturday night concerts at such places as the Cox Street Club in Coventry, or the Co-op Club in Nuneaton, there would be queues forming outside well before the doors opened.

The shows would be real, old-fashioned variety; there would be singers, jugglers and novelty acts such as Tina Day, who tap-danced on dinner plates. However, with Billy the audience got two turns for the price of one. Coming out in the first half, he would wear a glamorous evening gown, with fishnet tights and sparkly stiletto shoes. His face was made-up, including false eyelashes, but he never wore a wig. His own hair was simply shushed up in a short style, a la Judy Garland, and was sometimes dyed an auburn colour.

He would then sit on a high stool with his legs crossed and, in his own inimitable fashion, tell hilarious tales of venturing on trips with his close pal, Everard, along with episodes featuring Slack Alice and Apricot Lil.

One routine concerned a holiday to the seaside with Everard: "He loved the water – it was good for his war wound – and he was splashing about while I sat on a deckchair on the beach. Suddenly, Everard got into trouble with an octopus. 'Cut off his tentacles,' I shouted. Unfortunately, the lifeguard was a bit deaf..." He would also talk about going to the fair with Slack. "She loved the big dipper – and she's not alone..." And, in mentioning Slack's love of dancing, he would remark: "She was famous for her black bottom!"

There was a story about being on stage with Everard when they played both halves of a pantomime cow. "After the show, it was raining outside so we decided to walk home in the costume. I was at the front and Everard in the rear. As we crossed a field, I saw a bull pawing at the ground. 'What shall we do?' asked Everard. 'Well, I'm going to pretend to chew some grass – you'd better brace yourself...!'"

Another fictitious anecdote involved a visit to a fortune-teller: "She told me I would get a sign about my love life. In the dark, I stumbled against a dressing table – and the legs flew apart and the drawers fell down!"

For the second half of his act, Larry would be transformed, with his lipstick wiped off and his hair straightened, and he would walk on stage, in an immaculate suit and collar and tie, dragging his chair. He would then rest one hand onto the back of the chair, put his other hand on his hip and start regaling the audience with more tall stories, often nodding towards the pianist or someone in the crowd, with the comment: "I told you about it last night didn't I?" With perfect timing, he would add: "Remember, in bed..." before turning towards the audience to remark: "And he's got nits."

He would complain about being riddled with arthritis. He would look towards a club official, before glancing away to announce: "He's as common as dirt." He would say to someone in the front row: "How's your mother? Does she still keep ferrets? I thought so; I can smell 'em from 'ere."

At one club, the stage was a snooker table covered in a sheet and he remembers going to another venue which was so rough there was sawdust on the bar floor. He was interrupted by clanging bells during his turn at the Brassworkers, in Coventry, when a fire engine went past. Without taking a breath he said: "Sounds like my frocks have gone up in flames."

Billy once fell foul of the Club Secretaries Council, who ruled with a rod of iron. He was booked to appear at Edgwick Trades Hall Club in Coventry on a certain Saturday night but that same afternoon had to be in London to discuss plans for a summer show. He wrote to the club saying he would not be back in Coventry in time to appear and giving them the chance to find a replacement. As it happened, he arrived back in Nuneaton earlier than he expected and went out for a drink. He was seen and reported to the Secretaries Council. Billy was summoned to attend a disciplinary hearing at Cox Street Club when, because of his previous good record, and because he had lost his £3 10s appearance fee from Edgwick, he got off with a warning, which was put in writing.

One of his favourite dates was the Radford Social Club in

Coventry, where entertainments secretary Cec Barnes would pay him £12 for three weekend appearances.

The first time I saw my uncle on stage was at this club, when I was aged about twelve or thirteen. I remember thinking, "Why on earth is he wearing a dress?" I also couldn't quite understand why everyone in the crowded clubroom thought he was so outrageous. Obviously, at the time, the humour went right over my head. The most vivid recollection of that night, strange as it may seem, was being enthralled by a singer in a checked cowboy shirt yodelling.

Another of Billy's favoured venues was Cox Street WMC – known as the city's 'mother club' which, years later, was treated to a royal visit by the Queen. The ents sec there was Wal Jones, who knew he had a guaranteed full house when Billy occupied the popular Sunday lunchtime slot.

"The place would be packed with blokes and Wal used to say that they had heard all the dirty stories and filthy words in the factories all week and didn't want any of that sort of material. He said they wanted to see an artist, a performer who looks lovely and makes them laugh," Billy told me. "I was always naughty but never crude and never used bad language. I never talked about politics, religion or royalty. My act was built around everyday situations, without any offence to anyone."

Life back at Clifton Road was ticking along nicely. Dad Jim had by now retired, although Flo was still working part time at Courtaulds. Her sister May – my grandma – would visit most Saturdays, travelling over from Coventry by bus into town and then walking the rest of the way, via Queen's Road and the Cock and Bear bridge.

I used to join other members of the family who would congregate at Clifton Road on Sunday afternoons. Flo would climb onto a stool to reach a high cupboard in the front room – where she kept her 'stash' of tinned salmon and fruit and cream and we would all sit around for a traditional tea.

Billy would be at the centre of much light-hearted joviality, as he put a comic slant onto things he had seen and heard that week, mainly involving the antics of folk living in the street. His knack of making the simple, run-of-the-mill seem absurd invariably had us in fits of laughter.

Then, while Flo cleared away the tea things, my uncle would disappear upstairs and come back down, dressed in a suit and carrying a large brown suitcase. He was getting ready to go to work. It would be getting dark outside. There would be a knock on the door or the toot of a car horn and off he'd go, to fulfil a booking at some club or pub somewhere. It was a somewhat surreal and far from glamorous existence.

I clearly remember going along to watch him one Sunday night, at a large social club in the middle of Wolverhampton. My mum and dad took him in their car and I was allowed to join them, presumably because I had no school the following day. The smoke-filled venue was a sell out and I sat with pop and crisps in a games annexe. Every now and then I peeped through the door to see my uncle Bill standing in the spotlight on stage and people howling with laughter. It was an awe-inspiring image, which I've never forgotten.

In the summer of 1966 I started to be a very regular visitor to Clifton Road. After leaving Bablake School, I had been taken on as a junior reporter on the *Nuneaton Tribune* and my aunty Flo offered to cook my weekday lunch. I used to get a lift in a car with one of the printers, who lived in Stockingford and whose break coincided with mine. I would then sit at the kitchen table with my great granddad Jim and Bill while Flo served up a piping hot, meat-and-two-veg meal.

I gradually became intrigued to learn about my uncle's adventurous life as a full-time comedian. Sipping my dandelion and burdock pop and slipping into journalistic mode, I lapped up stories of what it was like 'in showbiz', how different audiences reacted and what mishaps were experienced by some of his fellow entertainers on the clubland circuit.

I was introduced to the music of Judy Garland; I was shown interesting articles and reviews in *The Stage* newspaper. I also quickly realised how much I shared my uncle's wicked sense of humour. Whatever he thought was amusing, similarly tickled me. I found myself totally on his wavelength; we had the same funny bone. We both loved Laurel and Hardy – and were likewise completely unmoved by Abbot and Costello. When I was in my teens, he took me one afternoon to the Palace Cinema in Queen's Road to see *Monsieur Hulot's Holiday*, a highly visual comedy starring Jacques Tati. It was the funniest film I'd ever seen and for years after we would have a private chuckle between ourselves recalling some of the scenes, such as 'The Strollers' and the squeaking dining room door.

Around the same time, in the mid-60s I went to Chapel End Liberal Club, one Sunday lunchtime, to watch my uncle in action. From my vantage point, perched on a windowsill at the very back of a packed concert room, I was witness to an event which left an indelible impression.

It took place in front of a raucous, beer-swilling crowd, made up mainly of local pitmen who applauded heartily when the compere announced: "Please give a big hand for today's turn – the one and only Billy Breen." Ronnie Hollis was at a piano at the side of the stage and played the introduction, as the star of the show came out, dragging a stool and wearing a full-length silk gown, slashed to the thigh above glittery high heels.

His opening line: "I've gone all limp," was greeted with cheers and what followed can only be described as a masterclass display. Billy Breen had the audience, quite literally, in the palm of his hand. He poked fun at Ronnie, who remained totally expressionless; he picked on the bar staff, the committee, the doorman and, in fact, anyone who took his fancy. Following the bingo-interval, he returned in a shiny, well-cut suit and continued with a string of side-splitting stories, as he stood with one hand leaning against a chair and the other resting on his hip. It was past three o'clock – over an hour after drinking-up time – when he finally left the stage, to a rip-roaring ovation. What a shame such a classical performance was not captured for posterity. If only we'd had iPhones in those days!

Meanwhile, back at Clifton Road, I would get the opportunity to meet an assorted array of characters, whose visits would coincide with my lunch breaks. There was Reg Needle from Leicester, with his tightly-belted raincoat and nervous twitch, who would talk non-stop about anything to do with film musicals, in particular Judy Garland. A man called Ernie Betteridge, who was an old family friend, used to cause amusement by the way he could magically produce a boiled sweet from his pocket and pop it straight into his mouth, avoiding the excuse to offer them around. Fellow showbiz artists would drop by, including a highly excitable pair who did a life-sized puppet act and a slim, young Australian drag artist who dissolved into tears when he confessed how he had been booed off stage at some Black Country working men's club the night before.

There was a girl, whose name I think was Shelly, who had met my uncle at a club and was eager to get into the acting profession. One lunchtime she was in the back room at Clifton Road, giving a rendition of an audition piece she was learning. Shelly was in full, dramatic voice and going quite over the top when Flo, standing at the sink doing the washing up, suddenly interrupted her. "Ssh," she said. "Dad's asleep upstairs." The girl halted in mid-sentence – and me and Bill fell about in hysterics.

Also, of course, I got to hear all about the odd-ball activities of some of the neighbours. In those days, it was rare for houses to have private phones. Because of the nature of his work, Billy needed to be directly contactable, so he had a phone installed – the only one in the street. His number was Nuneaton 4329 and the black, old-fashioned receiver stood on a small table in the neat front room. It not only gave Billy a lifeline for bookings and contact with agents such as Joan Davis from Coventry, but also provided a magical source of material to be woven into his act.

Friends in the street were told they were welcome to use the phone, as long as they put tuppence in a cardboard box next to it. What they didn't realise was that when they made their calls Billy was in easy earshot, just the other side of a curtain, which divided the parlour and the back kitchen.

He explained: "These dear ladies would get on the phone and seemed to be obsessed with their health, so that's how I got the bits about my aches and pains. One woman used to come in every day to call her daughter and would always start the conversation with 'I've not been well again'. She would then spend the next five minutes describing her migraine or some other illness problem. To hear her talk it was a miracle she was still alive. She would always end with 'I'll try to phone you tomorrow, if I'm well enough'. She was the one who said she wrapped her legs in tin foil to prevent arthritis and that's where that came from. Someone else suggested the advantages of using Fiery Jack ointment, which also found its way into my act."

Number 52 Clifton Road was like an open house. As well as using the phone, people would enjoy popping in and having a chat. One lad – Batho – had the strange habit of continually staring at his bare arms as he talked, while another neighbour was always going on about her husband who would roll back from the pub and then start 'clawing himself' as he lay on the front room carpet.

The Hoods lived over the road – and Billy was astonished when he heard they had named their new-born son Robin. "Just imagine, when he's older, if he gets stopped by the police and asked his name. How are they going to react when he says 'Robin Hood' especially if he happens to be in Nottingham at the time?"

For Billy, it was like having a real-life sit-com on his doorstep, which he absorbed and incorporated into his stage act. His wit was as sharp as a razor and he caught every tiny detail of people around him; their mannerisms, the way they talked and what they wore.

He had a thing about shoes; always insisting his own were kept brightly polished and well-heeled. The first thing he noticed about anyone was what they had on their feet. He would often whisper to me: "Clock the bats," – which meant, "Take a look at those shoes." As an avidly smart dresser himself he would just as instantly focus on people's clothes. "Love the frock, dear," he would casually remark. Or he might comment: "Her hat's fighting against that coat," when a passer-by just didn't look right. He would also say: "She obviously hasn't got a full-length mirror in her house." Another one of his comments, in wet weather, was: "Anybody not wearing a raincoat today doesn't own one."

While he was always a big draw on the local club scene, the dream of achieving more widespread fame seemed more distant than ever. Then, Billy's personal life was rocked by the sudden deaths of two people very close and dear to him.

Among the regular callers to Clifton Road was Billy's real mother, Ethel, who would travel by bus from Barwell about once a month. It was during one of her visits, on 2 March, 1963, that tragedy struck when Ethel had a stroke and died. This particular afternoon she had said to Billy: "I feel a bit tired. I think I'll go and have a little lie down." She went upstairs to the back bedroom Billy shared with his elderly dad, Jim, in the two-up-two-down house.

After a while, Billy went to see how Ethel was and, to his horror, found her stone cold. He was absolutely distraught. To his knowledge she hadn't been ill and the fact that she had died without warning while lying on his own bed, was almost too much for him to take in. Only a handful of mourners attended the funeral, on a cold, drizzly day, when Ethel was buried in the family grave at Nuneaton's Oaston Road cemetery, alongside Alice Hammonds, Billy's foster mum.

It was only after her death that Billy revealed to me that the woman I had known as his aunty Ethel was, in fact, his real mother. He quietly related the story of being 'advertised in a paper and put on a train as a baby to be adopted by the Hammonds'.

He once confided: "Adoption is not right. It is not fair on the people who accept such children into their homes. They don't know what they are taking on. The genes are different, you see." It was a poignant thing to hear from someone who was never 100 per cent certain of his own background, who was never officially adopted and who never met his real father. The fact that he loved Flo and

Jim is undeniable – but, lurking in the back of his mind was the constant stigma of being given away into the care of strangers.

Not long after the loss of Ethel there was further upset for Billy when Jim had to have a leg amputated. An old foot injury from a pit accident had turned gangrenous and Jim, at the ripe old age of eighty-seven, went into George Eliot Hospital for an operation. I remember calling round one lunchtime and finding Billy down the bottom of the garden in tears. "Dad's got to lose his leg," he said. "I just don't know what we're going to do."

As it happened Jim came through the ordeal marvellously, delighting in showing all and sundry his neat wound. Jim had a wheelchair and I enjoyed pushing him up to the Black Swan for a pint, with poodle Peter trotting alongside. He would also shuffle along in the garden tending to his patch of home-grown vegetables. Sadly, a year later, Jim suffered a fatal stroke, as he sat on the settee at home. It was another crushing blow to Billy, who again stood at the graveside in Oaston Road, his eyes red with sorrow, his shoulders hunched.

Despite feeling rock-bottom, Billy bravely battled on. He even fulfilled a club date on the night of Jim's funeral, in the grand tradition of 'the show must go on'.

But grief and despair began to have an effect on his own health. He developed stomach problems and tried to dull the pain by smoking more heavily than normal and going over the top with measures of gin and tonic. For the first time in his life, Billy experienced black moods and was on the verge of a nervous breakdown. It was sad to see him being so unnaturally subdued. A light had definitely gone out in his life and he even began to turn down bookings.

Billy refused to see a doctor, claiming he just had a bit of indigestion and in October, 1969 he collapsed in agony, at home in Clifton Road, while Flo was out shopping.

Luckily, his niece Joyce Malyon, who was then a district midwife, just so happened to pay a visit – and discovered an ashen-faced Billy sprawled on the floor in pools of blood. She called an ambulance and he was rushed into Manor Hospital for an immediate six-pint transfusion. He had suffered three burst stomach ulcers and for several days was quite ill.

Poor old Flo was beside herself. With her dad gone and Billy now in hospital, she became a lost soul. But, despite her poorly hip, Flo managed to make the journey every day to the hospital, hobbling along Manor Court Road to take clean pyjamas and bottles of Lucozade for the patient who she still regarded as her little boy. Before long, Billy gradually recovered and Flo knew he was getting better by the way he resumed chiding and teasing her – while at the same time keeping all the patients and staff on Nason Ward entertained.

Two of the nurses who looked after him appeared on his *This Is Your Life* programme. Helen Turner and Sue Cox were introduced by Eamonn Andrews and nervously walked out, wearing 70s-style maxi-dresses. "He was a great laugh. Even though he was so ill, he still kept everyone else happy," said Helen.

Billy went back home to Clifton Road to recuperate. He had passed his forty-sixth birthday and became very forlorn, wondering what the future had in store. The answer came with a phone call, out of the blue. On the other end of the line was entrepreneur Peter Dulay, who was compiling a line-up for a revue show at the Theatre Royal in Stratford, East London.

"It was an all-drag cast but I needed a compere to link it all together," said Peter. "I remembered seeing this very funny man, Larry Grayson, in Brighton a few years before, whose camp style would be ideally suited. It took me some time to track him down and I asked him to come and see me at my office in Wardour Street, which he did. I then offered him a two-week booking. He went on to be such a hit that he stayed for the full ten-week run and I became his manager."

Fate had certainly intervened for the rediscovered comic, who never again worked as Billy Breen. He said: "I don't really know why I said yes to Peter. But, since my illness, I hadn't worked and I had no bookings in my diary, so I just decided on impulse to give it a go. It's strange how things work out, but someone, somewhere, must have been watching over me."

The show, at the old Victorian music hall in the East End, was called *The Gaiety Box Revue* and featured some internationally-renowned female impersonators, such as Jean Fredericks and Rogers and Starr. It was all sequins and feathers and near-the-knuckle routines, with sketches written by Peter Dulay. But the whole production was upstaged, lock stock and barrel, by Larry Grayson. He was the only one on stage in a suit rather than a frock – and every night, he had the audience in fits of laughter, as he complained about his ailments, the dust in his dressing room and his fellow artists "who are all anybody's for a doughnut."

He would moan about his aches and pains: "Two weeks ago, I got it all down my right side. Last week it had moved to my left. I can't wait for next week, can I?" He would say he was "as limp as a vicar's handshake" and reveal that he always felt queer "when there's an 'r' in the month." He would stop in mid-sentence, rub his nose and say, "I think I've got worms." He would recommend having a lie down with a glass of Wincarnis (tonic wine) and two fairy cakes.

The show was such a success that Larry phoned me at work to invite me to go down to see it. I went with a colleague, Colin Webster, in his car, and we set off straight from work on a Friday afternoon, eventually arriving at the old-fashioned Stratford East theatre just before curtain-up. Tickets were waiting for us at the box office – and we then sat, wide-eyed and innocent, among a flamboyant audience; men with painted fingernails and face make-up and women with close-cropped hair and pencilled-on moustaches. The whole night was an experience to behold for two teenage lads from plain old Nuneaton. After the show, we went backstage – and Larry introduced me to one of the cast. "This is my nephew," said Larry. The reply was accompanied by a cheeky wink: "Yes, they all say that."

Larry became the most talked about entertainer in London. People were asking, "Where has this new boy come from?" Agents were beating a path to the Theatre Royal to catch this limp-wristed, eyebrow-raising comic, who didn't tell jokes, who made fun out of himself, his fellow cast members and his surroundings and who was simply outrageous.

Top impresario Paul Raymond immediately booked Larry for another drag show, *Birds of a Feather* at the Royalty Theatre in the West End. It starred Ricky Renee and Terry Durham – and Larry was billed as 'England's Comedy Sensation'.

From then on, doors swung open for Larry, as his career took off big style. "The timing was just right, for the business and for me," he said. "I was lucky to be seen by the right people at the right moment in my life. I was being called an overnight star – but it had taken me ninety-five years to get there."

CHAPTER 5
PALLADIUM DEBUT;
DREAM COMES TRUE

The summer of 1970 saw Larry at the Theatre Royal in Brighton for the season, with Arthur Askey, Kathy Kirby and Hetty King. Established performer Dora Bryan lived in the town and went to see a matinee with her children, which led to her and Larry striking up a close friendship.

"This fella walked on stage with a chair and started talking about the muck and the draughts in the theatre," said Dora. "My children kept telling me to be quiet because I was laughing so much. After the show I asked the theatre manager to take me backstage to meet Larry, who was so lovely and told me he was a big fan of mine. I asked him if he would like to be in my pantomime at the same theatre that Christmas and he replied, 'Oh, that would be nice.' I asked the management to write a part for him and they suggested that me and Larry do it ourselves, so we arranged to meet up at my house the next day.

"When Larry walked in, I told him I had been ill with a bad back. 'Don't start,' he said. Then he asked if I was wearing a vest and told me to get a copper bracelet. He lifted up his sleeve and showed me his wrist – which was green from a copper bracelet. Anyway, we had a lovely afternoon, chatting away, without ever getting down to writing a script. It didn't matter, because during the panto Larry never said the same thing twice. But we had so much fun and became such really good friends."

Just before starting rehearsals for *Goldilocks and Three*

Bears at Brighton, Larry got a phone call from manager Peter Dulay that made the hairs on the back of his neck stand up. He was told: "You're going to The Palladium."

This theatre, tucked away in Argyll Street, between Regent Street and Oxford Circus, dates back to 1910 and became famous as 'the ace variety venue of the world'. It was designed by Frank Matcham on the site previously occupied by Henglers Grand Cirque and the National Ice Skating Palace.

All the greatest showbiz stars had trod the Palladium stage, including Larry's beloved Judy Garland. One of his favourite film clips was from *I Could Go on Singing*, when Judy played a singer and stood nervously in the Palladium wings, waiting to make her entrance.

Now, unbelievably, Larry was being given the chance to actually stand in those same footsteps. It really was a dream come true. From Fife Street Working Men's Club to The Palladium. It had taken thirty-three years to come this far. To appear here was every entertainer's ambition.

As soon as he put the phone down after Peter Dulay's call, Larry called me at the *Nuneaton Evening Tribune* office. "You'll never guess what," he said, excitedly. "I'm going to the Palladium. There's a story for you."

Larry was booked to open on 30 November, 1970 for a two-week run. The variety show starred singer Peter Noone, from Herman's Hermits, and also included Australian balladeer Roger Whittaker, pianist Russ Conway, TV comedian Dick Emery and American dance pair The Clark Brothers. Larry was to appear second on the bill, immediately after the curtain-raising, high-kicking chorus girls.

"To play The Palladium was the absolute pinnacle of our business. Once you had stepped onto that amazing stage you knew you had made it," he said. "I'll never forget that first Monday morning when I walked into the theatre. Mr Brooks, who had been manager of the Liverpool Empire, where I had played many years before, came down from the stalls and said: 'Well, Larry, you are finally here. It's taken longer than we thought but you are here now.'

"When I stood on that stage I thought of all the great artists who had been here – Judy, Danny Kaye, Jack Benny, George Burns. Now it was my turn. It was a very emotional feeling – and one never to be forgotten."

In the show, Larry was introduced by compere Pete Murray and walked out with his chair. Seven minutes later he closed his act to thunderous applause. His dressing room was right at the top of the spiral staircase, next to the chorus girls. It was tiny but to Larry it was like being in heaven. Good luck messages were stuck on his mirror and Larry posed with a champagne glass – filled with water – for photographer Barry Woodward, from the *Tribune*, who had travelled down with me to cover the opening night.

Larry was on cloud nine and as he made his way out of the stage door he was stopped in his tracks by Wee Georgie Wood – a legendary, pint-sized, old-time performer – who told him: "You are very funny. You will go far."

Some friends from Nuneaton were in the audience and two of them – who ran a hotel at Astley Castle – asked Larry to go with them to a nightclub. Me and Barry were invited as well. We all piled into a taxi and arrived in a back street in Soho and went down some steps to a seedy-looking club. A peep-hole in the door opened and we were let in, to be greeted by a jaw-dropping sight. There were slim athletic-looking men, in tight, white trousers, dancing cheek-to-cheek with big, burly naval types. There were same-sex couples cuddling and kissing in dark corners. It was, so obviously, a gay venue. We sat against one wall, while our hosts went to the bar, and Larry turned to me

and said: "Don't you dare go to the toilets on your own."
Me and Barry were rooted, uncomfortably, to the spot.

After a short while, Larry decided it was time to leave.
We shared a cab back to Euston, just in time to catch the
late paper train to Nuneaton. The incident was never
again mentioned, but it left a firm impression on me – a
twenty-year-old wet-behind-the-ears lad who never knew
such places existed.

For the two-week run at The Palladium, Larry travelled
down to London every day from Nuneaton, catching the
3.50 p.m. and returning at midnight. As a result of his
success, the bookings rolled in, with a week's cabaret
engagement at the Cresta Club in Solihull and a call to
make his television debut on the Leslie Crowther *In Town*
show.

In the summer of 1971 Larry found himself back on the
south coast for a season at the Festival Theatre, Paignton,
as fourth on the bill behind Leslie Crowther, John Hanson
and Basil Brush. During twelve sun-blessed weeks, Larry
rented a flat overlooking Brixham harbour and Flo moved
down to stay with him for what was, incredibly, her first
proper holiday. She had only ever been away from home
on day trips, when she used to take young Billy on the
charabanc from Nuneaton to Blackpool or Skegness. This
was a completely new adventure for Flo, which she
thoroughly enjoyed. The flat was above a gift shop, Studio
66, and had beautiful views of the quayside, where Francis
Drake's ship *The Golden Hind* was docked as a tourist
attraction.

It was during this idyllic summer that Larry was given
the first hint that even better times might be just around
the corner. His performances in the Paignton show were
receiving impressive reviews in the trade and local press
but it was a visit to a local clairvoyant that finally

underscored his destiny.

"I was walking along the seafront one afternoon, with some of the cast, when I saw a booth advertising a fortune teller. Her name was Madame Credo and because I love that sort of thing, I decided to walk in. It was on a whim – but she looked straight at my hand and gave a gasp. 'It's wonderful. I'm elated,' she said. 'Oh, you have worked hard and you've had setbacks. But it's all going to change.' She said that within a year I would be at the top of whatever profession I was in and be a household name."

When Larry came out and told the other boys what she had said, they laughed it off. One remarked that the only way Larry could be a household name would be to change it to Brillo. But every word of Madame Credo's prediction came true. He said: "I did not believe it for one second but it happened, just like she said. By the following summer I was a nationwide star."

Larry had a very spiritual side to his nature and Madame Credo wasn't the only clairvoyant he had consulted. Back in the early 1950s he paid a visit to a fortune teller in Leamington Spa who said that his life would dramatically change for the good in a year containing the figure seven. He waited for it to happen in 1957, but nothing. Then in 1967, again no luck. But in the 1970s, he struck gold.

Larry firmly believed in life after death. He was convinced his mother Ethel visited him one night in his bedroom, where she had died. "I was still in mourning but suddenly I saw her standing by my bed, as clear as anything," he told me. "She looked so nice and peaceful and told me everything was going to be all right. It gave me a lovely feeling and I stopped grieving for her, there and then."

Many years later, when he was living at the bungalow in Harcourt Gardens, Larry had a social visit from a

Bedworth-born medium, Mark Brandist. In mid-conversation, Mark suddenly told Larry: "I've just had a vision, something to do with a ring and I'm getting a message that you must repair it and wear it."

Larry did no more than go straight into his bedroom and return with a small, broken gold ring. "This was my mother's, which had to be snapped to get it off her finger after she had died," he explained. "That was almost twenty-five years ago and I've kept it in a jewellery box ever since. I've never told a soul. This must be a message from my mother." I was in the room at the time and was stunned. The next day, Larry took the ring to a jeweller's in town, had it repaired and widened and wore it himself from then on.

There was even what you might call a possible spiritual connection shortly after Larry's death. Manager Paul Vaughan was in a taxi travelling through Bermondsey in London, to visit *The Stage* newspaper offices to place an obituary notice. It was drizzling. There were dark clouds overhead. Then, as the cab stopped at a set of traffic lights, Paul's eye was caught by the name over an Indian restaurant, 'Shefali'. As it happened there was a weather girl on BBC Midlands TV called Shefali Oza and, for some odd reason, Larry had always been gently amused whenever she appeared on screen. The name just stuck a chord with him. "The great Shefali," he used to call her. As Paul looked at the restaurant banner, his sad mood lifted and gave way to a wry smile. "That's typical of Larry – to send me a sign to cheer me up," he said.

Back in November 1971, Larry was again at the Palladium, twelve months after his debut. This time he was higher up a bill topped by Val Doonican and was given a ten minute spot. He stayed in the capital with a booking two weeks later at the Stork Club, a late night cabaret room, which was frequented by fellow artists and "anyone who's anyone in the business."

Peter Hepple, a celebrated writer with The Stage newspaper, reviewed Larry's act. He wrote: 'There is little doubt he has taken the West End by storm, with a style of confidentially camp delivery that has been honed to a precise edge. Whether being insulting about the surroundings in which he is working, reminiscing over his career in musical comedies – 'I refused the Chocolate Soldier' – telling of his day with the hunt or an encounter with the gypsies, Larry is achingly funny and never more so than when complaining of his miscellaneous pains.'

Larry's year ended with yet another London triumph – this time as the star of a revue at a nightclub in Hanover Square, owned by top female impersonator Danny La Rue. "I had heard lots of great things about Larry and went to see him in *Birds of a Feather*. I hated that show but he stood out like a beacon and I loved his act," said Danny. "I had my club and was also appearing at the Palace Theatre and the Prince of Wales and doing TV and radio and had not had a break for nine years. My manager said I needed to get away and I replied that I would only do so if he could get Larry Grayson to look after the show at my club. The deal was done and Larry was a tremendous success. You see, he was outrageous without being sleazy. He was a high camp performer of the highest calibre, who was clean and very funny."

Danny La Rue had also been around the business for many years before achieving fame. He had been a down-the-bill drag act in post-war reviews but became a star, renowned for his glamorous gowns and wigs. He had mentioned the up-and-coming Larry as "a name to watch out for" when I interviewed him at a press conference for the Coventry Theatre Birthday Show. A year later, Danny was asking my uncle to take the helm at his London club. This endorsement now made Larry the talk of the business.

Despite being forty-eight, he was hailed as 'the new boy from the Midlands', a star very much in ascendancy, whose talent was quickly being noted by the moguls of the small screen. Michael Grade, nephew of perhaps the country's top impresario, Sir Lew Grade, made a personal visit to watch Larry in action and immediately signed him up for a new TV talent show.

Saturday Variety went out at the beginning of January. Larry was scheduled to appear in the first three shows. His opening-night performance started with the words: "I think I've come to the wrong place. I thought I had a ticket to watch *The Generation Game.*"

That proved to be quite a prophetic observation, because nine years later he was to host that very show from the same studios. Larry went on to moan: "Look at the muck in 'ere," and after glancing sideways to say, "shut that door," the impact of his act was immediate.

Newspapers the following day were full of reviews about the national arrival of 'the new funnyman from the Midlands – and he was signed as the resident comedian on *Saturday Variety* for all sixteen weeks. By the middle of 1972, Larry Grayson was a household name throughout the country – just as Madame Credo had predicted.

CHAPTER 6
WHIRLWIND RISE TO FAME

The public reaction to his appearances on *Saturday Variety* made Larry Grayson the hottest property in show business, with offers flooding in from all over the country. He shared the bill at Bexhill-on-Sea with former chart-topping singer Frank Ifield and made two television appearances from ATV's Birmingham studios – doing a walk-on part in the popular teatime soap opera *Crossroads* and being introduced by Norman Vaughan as a guest on the live Sunday evening game show *The Golden Shot*.

Larry adopted a signature tune – *The Man That Got Away*, appropriately from Judy's *A Star is Born* film – and soon his catchphrase "Shut That Door" was on everyone's lips. The line had come into his repertoire in accidental fashion when he was at Paignton during the 1971 summer season. Also in the show was a singer called Heathmore and he used to tell Larry how, whenever his manager wanted to have a private word with him in the dressing room she would always say: "Now, before we start, shut that door." Heathmore explained: "This one night, Larry was on stage and I was watching from the wings. He was doing his usual stuff about feeling the draught when he glanced at me and said 'Shut that door'. The audience collapsed with laughter and Larry kept that phrase in his act from then on."

Larry's whirlwind rise to fame brought lots of sudden changes to his life, including the purchase of his first ever car; a bronze-coloured Chrysler 180, which he bought from Parker's garage in Edward Street. Initially, my dad, Reg Malyon, was enlisted to be Larry's driver and several other friends later followed suit.

The car was soon being well used to whizz Larry here, there and everywhere. On the first Thursday after he'd got the keys, it was being driven to Thames Television studios at Teddington Lock, London, where Larry was to be a guest on the *Mike and Bernie Winters Show*. Two days later, the Chrysler was making its way to ATV's Elstree Studios, for *Saturday Variety*. Then, on the Monday, two days later, it was another Nuneaton-London journey, this time for a Royal Gala at the Palladium.

Larry had been invited to join a glittering, international line-up to raise money for the British Olympic Fund. The stars, to perform in front of the Queen, included Glenn Ford, Michael Caine, Liza Minnelli, Rowan and Martin and Roger Moore. The show was screened on TV the following weekend – with viewing figures of twenty-three million. Larry again received glowing reviews. His opening line was: "I'm dying to belch," which one newspaper critic said "had the audience laughing their tiaras off."

The producer was legendary impresario Sir Lew Grade and he was so pleased with Larry's performance that he sent him a personally-signed letter: "I have been especially asked to express the appreciation of Her Majesty the Queen and the Duke of Edinburgh to you for your contribution to the Royal Gala Performance which was such a success. I am, too, deeply grateful."

Larry was given his own weekly half-hour TV series *Shut That Door*, which was recorded at Elstree and featured various guest stars every week. The opening show had pianist Mrs Mills and gobbledegook language-master Stanley Unwin. Larry took part in sketches, answered fictitious letters from viewers in an agony-aunt spot and also introduced other characters, such as Everard Farquarharson's pal, Michael Bonaventure. There was a running gag during the series regarding musical director Jack Parnell and a lost brooch. *Shut That Door* ran for twelve weeks and built up Larry's ever-expanding fan-base.

He was booked to top a variety bill at the Savoy Theatre and followed it up by a week in cabaret at the equally prestigious West End establishment, The Café Royal. He was not due on stage until 11.00 p.m., so used to travel down from Nuneaton just after watching the six o'clock news. On the first night, as he made his way out of the door, Flo said: "Here you are Bill, I've made you a flask and some fish paste sandwiches for later."

He replied: "How can I possibly walk into the Café Royal, of all places, with a Thermos and a packet of sandwiches in my hand?"

During that week, Larry did not return home until way past 3.00 a.m. – and Flo would be sitting up, every night, waiting for him.

Sometimes, especially when he appeared at the top London venues, there would be lavish caviar-and-crab buffets laid on in Larry's dressing room, with the compliments of the management. But he was never one for exotic or fancy food. At home, he was happy with Flo's plain, run-of-the-mill meals. Larry liked egg and chips, sausage batches, pork dripping on fresh crusty bread and roast chicken. His favourite snack was melted cheese on a plate.

Even when he was earning a fortune, he never lived the champagne lifestyle – and actually hated drinking the bubbly stuff. Larry would often be presented with expensive bottles of Moët, which he would give away to friends, or leave in the bottom of the fridge.

In September 1972, Larry moved home, reluctantly swopping his cosy abode in Clifton Road for an imposing detached property in Hinckley Road, on the other, 'posher' side of Nuneaton. He said: "My manager insisted that it was not right for such a big star to live in a terrace house. I loved Clifton Road; I had been there for years and knew all the neighbours. But, in the end, I accepted the advice and paid £15,000 – with a mortgage – to buy 85 Hinckley Road, which was opposite the college and even had a flagpole in the front drive. It was a lovely house, with a massive garden at the rear and Flo just couldn't believe how much space we now had, for just us two and our pet poodle, Peter. It meant we had to employ a cleaner and a gardener but we also added a bar, next to the lounge, with proper padded stools and optics, where we had some great family parties."

The new house was called The Garlands – in tribute to Judy, obviously – and pride of place in the hallway was a photograph taken at the end of the Royal Gala, with Larry bowing gracefully as Her Majesty shook his hand. There were soon other mementos to adorn his shelves, as Larry collected a trophy from the *TV Times*, whose readers voted him the funniest man on the box, while his colleagues in The Grand Order of Water Rats presented him with a mounted silver rat, as their Television Personality of the Year.

During the year Larry turned his talents to singing, with the release of an LP record *What A Gay Day*. Among the twelve tracks were such titles as 'My Friend Everard', 'I've Got It Here', 'Just a Gigolo' and, of course, 'Shut That Door', which was also brought out as a single. The album, on the York label, is now considered a collectors' item and often appears up for auction on the eBay site. During his career, Larry also recorded three other singles, 'Oh What a Pretty Face' on Pye, 'Who's Stuffing Your Turkey This Christmas?', which United Artists released as a novelty record in December 1975, and a cringe-inducing song about Terry Wogan on Monarch, backed by the Mike Sammes singers, which came out in 1983.

Meanwhile, a magical year swung to a close with a record-breaking week at Caesar's Palace in Luton and Larry took out a two-page ad in *The Stage*, wishing everyone 'A Very Merry Xmas and 365 Gay Days for 1973'.

But there was still one more spectacular event to round off an amazing, whirlwind twelve months when, on 17 December, Eamonn Andrews uttered those immortal words: "Larry Grayson – tonight, this is your life."

The announcement – regarded as a televisual rubber-stamp for personal achievement – came as a complete surprise to Larry, who admitted: "I thought the roof had fallen in." He had just finished recording a Christmas Special and was thanking the Thames Studio audience when Eamonn crept up behind him, clutching the famous red book, and tapped him on the shoulder.

The *This Is Your Life* programme makers had decided, almost three months previously, to make Larry a 'victim' and had then launched into one of their usual top-secret missions. My mum, Joyce, was contacted and enrolled into helping the researchers put together the Larry Grayson story. She was sworn not to tell a soul and was told: "If Larry gets wind of what we're doing, even at the last minute, the show will be scrapped."

The instructions and the secrecy caused Mum more than a few problems. Phone calls from the production crew to her home had to be quickly curtailed if anyone else walked into the room. "I'm sure my husband Reg thought I was having an affair," she said later. "He kept saying, 'who was that you were talking to?' and I just had to reply 'oh, just someone about work.' I also had to have meetings, without anyone knowing, with some of the researchers and this also led to some odd looks from people who knew me and were obviously wondering why I was sitting in a café in my midwife's uniform whispering to a couple of strangers."

Gradually, as D-Day approached, various family members and friends, who were going to be asked to take part in the show, were let in on the secret but still things had to be kept strictly hush-hush. Even code words were used in what became like something from a James Bond movie.

Flo was kept completely in the dark – until the day that Larry had left to go to the studios to rehearse his Christmas Special. She was then told by my mum what was happening and was helped to hurriedly pack her clothes for the exciting trip to London and to appear on television.

This Is your Life was scheduled to be recorded the following day. The friends-and-family cast included my mum and dad, Flo, her sister, May, and husband, Charlie, Alf and Nell Freeman and Harry Leslie. Along with other family members, including myself, we all travelled first class, at Thames Television's expense, on the train from Trent Valley Station to Euston. From there we were picked up in chauffeur-driven cars to be taken to a four-star hotel at Hampstead Heath, to stay and prepare for the show.

Scripts were produced, read-throughs took place, food and drink was laid on and then everyone departed for the studios, where, in a cloak-and-dagger operation, we were smuggled into locked-off rooms behind the scenes.

Before setting off, I had confided to my *Tribune* editor, Eric Myatt, about what was being planned. I then wrote a story, revealing the town's best-kept secret – ready to be published as soon as the TV embargo was lifted.

After Larry had been 'captured' by Eamonn he was taken, in a daze, back to his dressing room, while preparations were made to record *This Is Your Life*. The Christmas Special set was changed and the audience stayed in their seats, waiting with bated anticipation for the proceedings to begin.

As a babe in arms, with foster-mum Alice Hammonds, shortly after arriving in Nuneaton

Above: Young Billy Hammonds (second row, left) with a group of children on Abbey Green

Below: With Flo in the lounge of their home in Hinckley Road

Baby William Sully-White, before he was taken from his Oxfordshire birthplace to be handed over to the Hammonds in Nuneaton

An early publicity shot of Larry Grayson after he had been signed by London agent Evelyn Taylor in the mid-1950s

In drag for his club act, with his hair styled like his idol, Judy Garland

The author's mum, Joyce Malyon, and his two sons, Marc and Ashley, with Larry during a charity event in Coventry

Celebrating his 70th birthday with a cake presented to him by local newspaper, the Nuneaton Tribune

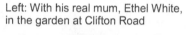

Left: With his real mum, Ethel White, in the garden at Clifton Road

All dolled up for a routine entitled "A Pretty Girl Is Like A Melody " at the New Pavilion in Redcar

A publicity photograph taken in the 1980s

With close members of his adoptive family, the Roberts Sisters, Barbara (left), Joan (right) and the author's mother Joyce

The man he called dad, Jim Hammonds, in a wheelchair after having a leg amputated

Above: Enjoying the trappings of success, although he never learned to drive

Below: A photo-call for a panto in Mansfield, with Jean Rogers, boxer Herol Bomber Graham and Dougie Clarke

The author, Mike Malyon (front left) and his mum's younger brother Mick Roberts, with their uncle Bill (back right), standing alongside a fellow clubland artist

Right: Flo (front, right) and elder sister May with their parents James and Alice Catcliffe. James was killed in the First World War and Alice died of cancer a few years later

Below: Larry was joined by aspiring actor Mark Barnsley, from Nuneaton, for the panto Aladdin at Mansfield

In a pensive mood during his early days on the local club circuit

Teaming up with Isla St Clair helped to make The Generation Game the most watched programme on TV

Relaxing at home in the 1950s

As Billy Breen (right) with a fellow performer, promoting the Radio Tymes summer show at Redcar in 1950

Grayson's Scandals at the London Palladium

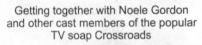

Getting together with Noele Gordon and other cast members of the popular TV soap Crossroads

Cutting the tape alongside civic guests at a function in Nuneaton

Having fun at a garden party at the Mary Ann Evans Hospice in Nuneaton

Visiting the mayor's parlour in Nuneaton with other family members, including Flo (second left) at the invitation of Councillor Albert Walker

Above: Lunch with staff from the Nuneaton and Bedworth Trader during a promotional tour with the newspaper group

Left: Always smartly dressed, on or off stage

Below: Helping volunteers on a charity stall during one of his many local public appearances

During a break in recording
"A Question of Entertainment"
at the BBC Studios in Manchester,
with Ken Dodd (left), Tom O'Connor
(right) and the author Mike Malyon

Dora Bryan became a close
friend, after she had invited
Larry to appear in her panto
in Brighton

Above: Hats off and on
horseback at the 1979
opening of the Riding for
the Disabled Centre in
Galley Common, Nuneaton

Left: With Rustie Lee and
Ian Lavender for the panto
in Leicester

Above: Giving his beloved Flo a hug
during a visit to her nursing home

Right: As a young boy, standing alongside
Jim Hammonds in front of the terraced
cottages on Abbey Green

The poster for the 1973
Coventry Theatre
Birthday Show

Advertising Aladdin at the
Civic Theatre, Mansfield

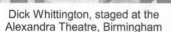

Dick Whittington, staged at the
Alexandra Theatre, Birmingham

CHAPTER 7
EAMONN SAYS:
THIS IS YOUR LIFE

As a breathless Larry settled into his chair for the telling of his life story, Eamonn opened the programme by saying: "Less than twelve months ago few knew your name, but now millions know it and your famous catchphrase "Shut That Door."

The Christmas Show guests, who had all been in on the secret, were introduced. Mike and Bernie Winters, John Hanson, Lionel Blair and Heathmore were followed onto the set by Rod Hull – whose Emu then proceeded to attack Larry, leaving him to gasp: "I'll kill that bird."

In any interviews, charting his rise to fame, whenever Larry had spoken about Flo, he gave her the affectionate nickname 'Fan'. And it was "Florence, known as Fan," who Eamonn next called to come from behind the curtain. Clearly emotional, Larry greeted 'the person closest to him' as she limped across the stage, carrying her handbag.

"You all right, love?" Larry whispered, as he clasped her hand.

Pointing towards Larry, Eamonn asked: "Is he very fussy to look after?"

Flo quietly replied: "He's not too bad."

Larry chipped in: "She wouldn't tell you anyway. She would never give away a secret."

Flo's sister, May, and her husband, Charlie, missed their cue before making their bow, to be followed by Alf and Nell Freeman, dressed to the nines in evening wear. My mum and dad, Joyce and Reg Malyon, told how they had taken Larry to a club in Warwick and had mistaken a private house for the stage door. "We walked in and realised our mistake when we saw this old lady getting ready for bed," recalled Joyce. "Larry said: 'It looks like we're in the wrong place,' and the woman replied 'I should think you are.' We quickly turned round and made our way out, suitcase first."

Dora Bryan talked about her friendship with Larry, before 'Student Prince' John Hanson demonstrated the proper way to swirl a cape. This came about because, as part of his act, Larry used to pretend he had performed in musicals: "I've been very busy. I've done *The Maid of the Mountains, The Quaker Girl and Rose Marie* – but I refused *The Chocolate Soldier.*"

The show ended with an eighty-year-old Harry Leslie recalling the bitterly-cold 1947 tour to Devon. As the closing credits rolled, to the sound of the 'Your Life' signature tune, Larry walked towards the camera, with Flo by his side and tears in his eyes, and said "I love you all."

With the programme in the can – and due to be screened ten days later – everyone involved, including the production crew, enjoyed a backstage party, along with other relatives and friends of Larry who had been in the audience. The celebrations continued when we returned to the Hampstead hotel, with Larry getting tipsy and looking forward to 'the best Christmas ever'.

One abiding memory I have of that night was seeing my granddad, Charlie Roberts, wandering along the plush-carpeted hotel corridor in his braces, with bottles clinking in a carrier bag, as he tried to find his room. To him and my nan, May, this was a taste of another world. For Charlie, who had worked as a delivery driver for Alfred Herberts, this was the first time he had been treated like a

VIP. He had just appeared on television, been wined and dined for free and was now heading to bed, ready to enjoy one last nightcap.

It was such a special occasion and Larry was deliriously happy as he sat with his adoring friends and family all around him. He kept pulling me to one side to whisper: "Your uncle is a star – you know that don't you?"

In the New Year, and throughout 1973, Larry went on to top the bill at all the major theatres in the country. He was at the Wellington Pier, Great Yarmouth, for the summer, on a bill that included comedy newcomers Cannon and Ball, before going to Margate, where he smashed all attendance records. Then, in October, he achieved another milestone by headlining the annual *Birthday Show* at Coventry Theatre.

"It had always been my dream, to play that theatre, ever since Flo had taken me there as a boy, when it was called the Hippodrome," he said. "In my club days, in trips to Coventry, whenever I went past the theatre I would look up and think "One day, I'll get there." I nearly did it in the 1950s, when Eve Taylor had booked me to appear at the Coventry Hippodrome, on a bill starring the singer Anne Shelton and comedian Derek Roy, who was then very big on radio's *Bandbox*. I was thrilled but then Miss Taylor called to say 'Sorry, Larry, you're not doing Coventry. Derek Roy does two spots in the first and second halves, so they do not want you.' That was a terrible disappointment. But then when I did finally get to Coventry Theatre, I topped the bill in my own show, which was marvellous."

Crowds flocked from all over the Midlands to watch a smash-hit variety production, directed by Dick Hurran. There was a full orchestra, the sixteen-girl Pamela Devis dancers, and acts such as pianists Rostal and Schaefer – complete with fountains and waterfalls on stage – the Kaye

Sisters, comedy magician Larry Parker and Rod Hull, with his Emu. Before the start of every performance, the stage manager would make an announcement to the cast, over the backstage speakers: "Tonight, ladies and gentlemen, we are playing to another full house."

Larry came out in the first half and also did a song-and-dance number with the Kaye Sisters, before closing the show with his stand-up routine. "I rocked the place and got a fantastic ovation every night," he said. "It was a beautiful show and I felt at home. It was very emotional. At the end, when I came out to thank the company and the audience, I would say 'I am now going to my dressing room and get myself ready to go back to Nuneaton, where I belong.' That did it."

All the family were in the first-night audience, going to Coventry in a coach. We had prime seats and the atmosphere was buzzing. But Flo was totally unimpressed and, actually, quite underwhelmed. Her only comment: "That was nice. I liked the dancers."

In a review in the *Coventry Evening Telegraph*, David Isaacs was more forthcoming. He wrote: 'You could say it with scores of superlatives. You could envelop it with unstinting praise. I'm prepared to start more simply by saying just this – last night was one of the most memorable evenings I have ever spent in a theatre.'

The article, headlined 'Larry's Comic Brilliance in Starry Show' continued: 'Show business has a manner of surrounding itself with trumped-up rags-to-riches stories. The word 'star' is brazenly used about third-rate nonentities who achieve only passing success. Some of us use the language more moderately. But star is a word one must now apply to Larry Grayson. He has a sense of style and a technique I have rarely seen surpassed. He has a comic timing born out of thirty years' experience. But the extra which Larry Grayson has can be summed up in a single word – warmth. The standing ovation he received from last night's audience was spontaneous and genuine. The atmosphere was charged with emotion. We probably all wanted Larry Grayson to be good. In the event, he wasn't good at all – he was brilliant.'

After a hugely lucrative eight-week run, Larry went straight from Coventry into the pantomime *Aladdin* at Bristol Hippodrome, which also featured Rod Hull and his Emu and Dilys Watling. As the year came to a close, he took part in a *Royal Gala Night*, attended by Princess Alexandra in aid of Romsey Abbey, which was staged at the Gaumont Theatre in Southampton.

The successes continued into 1974, when he followed up a spell at Bournemouth with another Dick Hurran spectacular, *Grayson's Scandals* at the ABC in Blackpool.

This was only his third appearance in Blackpool, which is known as the entertainment capital of the north. He was at the same venue for three nights in May 1972, with Peter Noone, Joe 'Mr Piano' Henderson and Moira Anderson, and years before he had been, in his own words, "in very small print" on a bill at the old Queen's Theatre. This time his show was being promoted as one of Blackpool's leading attractions – along with the Tower and the Pleasure Beach.

By now, Larry had a white Rolls Royce, with the registration LG 3, and needed a full-time chauffeur. Barry Moore, who lived with his wife and young family in Nuneaton, took on the job, which turned into being Larry's permanent on-the-road assistant, working not just as a driver but also as a dresser and general dogsbody. In addition, Barry became a useful helping hand for Flo, doing some of the cooking and shopping – and taking her in the Rolls to have her hair done.

For the season in Blackpool, Larry, Flo and Barry shared

a rented detached house, just off the seafront, which became a real home from home. Friends and family would visit and stop for weekends and the house, with its large entrance hall and galleried staircase, lent itself to being the venue for numerous after-show parties. It was a happy summer. The show, which featured The Kaye Sisters, Larry Parker, The Fredianis acrobats and ventriloquist Keith Harris, with Orville, was an eight-performances-a-week sell-out. On Sundays, Larry would be called on to attend various charity functions and benefit concerts, while he was also kept busy compiling a daily diary column in the *Blackpool Gazette*.

Entitled 'Grayson's Week', he talked about going to Fleetwood for the day – when he was surrounded by autograph hunters – and visiting the zoo – when everyone spent more time looking at him than the monkeys. He sought refuge in the restaurant and the sight of hundreds of fans peering through the windows had him admitting: "Now I know how the animals feel."

Larry did an hour-long Shut That Door TV special for London Weekend – and then, in October 1974, he took his *Grayson's Scandals* show to the Palladium.

This was, undoubtedly, his proudest moment. *Saturday Variety* had provided the breakthrough; the Coventry *Theatre Birthday Show* was something to cherish; *This Is your Life* had been an accolade. But for Larry to head his own show at the theatre of his dreams was like being handed the crown jewels.

"I will never, ever forget that feeling, as I stood, incognito and alone, in a shop doorway opposite the Palladium, staring up at the sign," said Larry. "It was the afternoon of my opening night and was drizzling with rain. My face and my name were blazoned right across the top of the theatre. I couldn't believe it. Then, when I walked round to the side entrance, the stage door keeper welcomed me. 'Let me show you to the No. 1 dressing room, Mr Grayson,' he said. Screwed onto the door was a brass plaque, with my name on it.

"When I went inside, I was overcome. All I kept thinking about was the list of stars that had occupied this very room. Now it was mine. I then walked along the small corridor to the side of the stage. I stopped in the wings and imagined my Judy, standing at that very spot. A shiver went down my back. Just like Judy, I was going to top the bill at The Palladium."

Once again, Dick Hurran had pulled out all the stops. As the curtain rose, Larry appeared on stage in a white vintage Rolls Royce, with his own chauffeur Barry Moore in the driving seat, wearing a white peaked cap. As Larry stepped out of the car, the theatre shook with applause, while cheers also rang out from the audience.

Sitting in the stalls, looking a bit bewildered by all the excitement, was Flo, surrounded by all the family who had travelled together from Nuneaton to London in a hired bus. Before going into the auditorium, I had hurried backstage, with May's son, Mick Roberts, to wish Larry the best of luck. All he wanted to hear was that Flo had arrived okay and was out front. At one stage during the show, Larry briefly glanced towards where he knew Flo was sitting and blew a kiss. It was an extraordinary, touching moment; a link between two people who had shared so many ups and downs, who had journeyed together so far, from that cobbled backyard in Abbey Green to this magnificent theatrical setting.

Noele Gordon joined a bill that also included ventriloquist Keith Harris, with Cuddles, plus French mime artist George Carl. During the show, Larry sang a duet with Noele – and as she left the stage he announced to the audience: "She's very old, you know. And she's deaf as a post." But it was all in good jest, because he and the former *Crossroads* star were very close friends. Once, as a publicity stunt, they even pretended to have got engaged. But, like Larry, Noele never married and lived with her mum in Ross-on-Wye. She used to send Larry a bunch of roses every Valentine's Day – and also, for a joke, issued him with a writ accusing him of slander because of his comments during the Palladium show. Larry had the properly drawn-up legal notice framed and hung behind the bar at his Hinckley Road home. He made his second appearance in *Crossroads* in 1975 when he played the part of a chauffeur, for the wedding of Noele's character Meg Richardson to Hugh Mortimer. I think that was the one-and-only time that my non-driving uncle ever sat behind a steering wheel.

Meanwhile, top theatre critic Jack Tinker was full of praise for the *Grayson's Scandals* production. He wrote in the *Daily Mail*: 'Like the best and the rarest of our comedians, Larry creates a special language from the whims of his own bizarre personality. How else could he simmer a Palladium audience to jelly merely by observing of his musical director: "He lives with a woman!" Life, he makes you feel, is full of cherry pips spat in his face. And he is quite capable of spitting them right back.'

After the heady success of the Palladium, Larry went into pantomime at Birmingham Hippodrome, in *Aladdin*, this time directed by Peter Dulay, with Alfred Marks joining Dilys Watling and Keith Harris in the cast.

The Birmingham show, which opened on Christmas Eve, meant that Larry was able to travel every day from Nuneaton. Once, he was going to the theatre along with Flo and May. They were all in the Rolls, being driven by Barry Moore, and as they pulled off the Bedworth by-pass, to go onto the M6, it started to snow. "Look at the weather," said Flo. To which May, unflinchingly replied: "Well, we are heading north." Larry fell about in the front seat.

While Flo was unmoved by Larry's success, May revelled in it. She would go up to complete strangers in the street and tell them: "Larry Grayson's my brother, you know," even if they were not the least bit interested. She would introduce herself in the same way to members of the audience or backstage crew at any of Larry's shows she went to. May shared her foster brother's warm sense of humour and was overwhelmed when he bought a house, opposite his own in Hinckley Road, for her and her husband, Charlie, to live in. They had lived for years in a poky cottage – with an outdoor lavatory and no bathroom – in Recreation Road, Coventry, which had been compulsory purchased to make way for a clinic. Now, the move to Nuneaton meant that May could call in on Larry and Flo every day. She would pop into town to do a bit of shopping for them and Larry used to eagerly watch out of his front window to see May's suede boots emerge from the platform of the bus on her return.

So, it was a real tragedy when, in 1975, May suffered a stroke, just a week before she was due to welcome eldest daughter, Joan, over on holiday from her home in Canada. My nan had been excitedly awaiting the visit, to show Joan for the first time the neat, semi-detached house that Larry had bought for her.

May was rushed into George Eliot Hospital where she lay in a coma as doctors diagnosed her condition as terminal. Joan was phoned and booked on the next plane out of Toronto. Me and my dad went to Heathrow to collect her and drove back in silence and sadness, direct to the hospital. Joan sat at May's bedside, held her hand and whispered: "I'm here, Mum." Within a matter of minutes, May passed away.

She was sixty-eight and had raised three daughters and a son in hard times when money was tight. Husband Charlie had a steady but modestly-paid job at the Alfred Herbert factory and supplemented his income by being a bookie's runner. In the days before licensed betting shops, he accepted wagers from workmates and neighbours, which he would then pass on to an illegal bookmaker based in Longford. When I visited my nan and granddad on Saturday afternoons, there would always be a stack of handwritten betting slips and little piles of money on the dining table, while a stream of people would be calling in to place their six penny or shilling bets. There was always the fear that the operation would be discovered by the police – but, looking back, I think it would be amazing if the authorities weren't already aware of what was going on, but chose to turn a blind eye.

May was a vastly different character to her sister, Flo. She was much more forthcoming, opinionated and domineering – with a cheerful personality. She was always the first to laugh out loud at Larry's stories, sharing his ability to see the funny side of everyday life. May was immensely proud of Larry's achievements and basked in the glory of her 'famous brother's' fame. The move to the house in Hinckley Road, barely 100 yards from where Larry and Flo lived, was the highlight of May's life. She was so looking forward to showing it off to Joan and the timing of her fatal stroke was bitterly cruel.

Larry insisted on paying for her funeral and her ashes were buried in the family plot at Oaston Road cemetery. Charlie remained in the Hinckley Road property for another twelve months before moving into sheltered accommodation in James Diskin Court in Attleborough –

next door to, would you believe it, Everard Court – where he remained until his death from cancer two years later.

Among the regular visitors to Larry's 'Garlands' home was a woman called Liz, a distant auntie and a real eccentric person who lived in the north Warwickshire village of Polesworth. She would arrive by bus once a week, carrying a bag full of bottles of fizzy pop. Larry had once remarked that he liked to put lemonade into vases of flowers to help them stay fresh longer and as Liz's son worked at a local mineral water company, she decided to take it on herself to deliver a regular supply. "Liz, I'm a big star – don't you think I can afford to buy a few bottles of pop?" Larry would say to her. But, no matter, she felt it was her duty.

We used to call her 'the great and powerful Liz' and would love to hear her talk about some of the things she had been up to in her younger days, such as how she once took off one of her stockings at the roadside to replace a fan-belt when a car she was travelling in broke down. She was quite a large woman and would sit on an upright chair with her legs wide apart as she chatted away – on one occasion incredibly claiming to have caught anthrax after going behind some hedges in a farm field with an admirer. Liz, like Flo, didn't have any sense of humour and couldn't understand why we would be collapsing in fits of giggles over her revelations. Needless to say, Flo also never got the joke – and would carry on pottering about in the background, making pots of tea and supplying plates of sandwiches.

For the next three years Larry criss-crossed the country, acclaimed as one of Britain's top crowd-pulling entertainers. On or off stage, he always made sure he was smartly dressed and the style of wearing his glasses on a chain around his neck became another one of his trademarks.

He had the distinction of being impersonated on TV by Mike Yarwood and was a regular guest on all the big chat shows, hosted by the likes of Terry Wogan, Michael Parkinson, Mike Aspel and Russell Harty.

He went to Jersey to appear in a charity gala, in front of Prince and Princess Michael of Kent. He appeared on television in popular game shows *Celebrity Squares* and *Blankety Blank*, donned music hall costume in *The Good Old Days*, recorded at Leeds' City Varieties Theatre, and in 1977 presented *The Larry Grayson Show* from London Weekend's South Bank studios, which featured his own pianist, Dennis Plowright and guest stars David Nixon, Neville King, The Bachelors, Brotherhood of Man and Bill Pertwee.

His list of catch-phrases and characters also expanded. Pop It In Pete, the postman, and Self- Raising Fred, the baker, were added to his retinue, along with expressions such as 'my hair needs washing' and 'I'm sweating like a dray horse'. Fingering the back of his head, he would look to the wings and add: "This place is alive."

Larry explained: "The names and phrases I use in my act are all based on real people and the stories come from actual circumstances. For instance, I was in the Post Office one day, when it was teeming down outside, and this woman came in, shook the rain off her coat and announced to all and sundry, 'What a gay day!' Another time I overheard these two women chatting at the bus stop. One was telling the other about her daughter's new boyfriend. 'He seems like a nice boy,' she said. So that's where I got those from."

Flo remained totally unfazed but became something of a celebrity herself, as magazines featured her as 'the woman behind Larry Grayson' and photographed her, doing the washing up or dusting the furniture, at the Hinckley Road 'big house', as she called it. She never ceased to amaze Larry with her incapacity to appreciate or acknowledge any of his achievements. When he told her that he was going to make his debut at The Palladium, she showed absolutely no interest and was more concerned about how many bags of coal to order from the coalman, as they always loved to have a real fire.

Once, she was telling Larry about a man who had asked after him in the street. Larry casually enquired: "Who was that then?"

Flo said: "That man with the glasses and the small dog."

Larry, puzzled, said: "I still don't know who you mean."

Flo replied: "Well, he knows you."

To which an exasperated Larry retorted: "Flo, the whole nation knows me."

Larry loved being a star and had spent five glorious years soaking up the adulation and all the rewards that went with it. He had fulfilled his aim; to get to the top. But what he didn't realise that his fame was to get even higher. A phone call in 1978 led to Larry dramatically raising his profile, as well as his bank balance.

CHAPTER 8
TOPPING TV CHARTS
AS GEN GAME HOST

"Flo, you'll never guess what – I've been asked to do *The Generation Game*," Larry said as he walked into the dining room after putting down the phone.

"Well, you know we never see that programme," was Flo's honest reply. "We always watch the other side."

It so happened that also in the room on this particular day, in April 1978, was my mum, Joyce. Her reaction to Larry's news was more positive. "You must take it," she urged. Within a week, virtually every newspaper in the land was announcing in big headlines that Larry Grayson was being handed one of the top programmes on TV.

The Generation Game was a hugely popular Saturday evening game show that had been hosted for six years by Bruce Forsyth, who had now decided to swop channels. The BBC were contemplating scrapping the series, but Billy Cotton, head of light entertainment, suggested inviting Larry to take it over and producer Alan Boyd went along with the idea. "I knew it was a gamble," said Larry. "But I also reckoned that if the BBC were prepared to give it a go then so was I. They told me I could do it my way, exactly how I wanted. I said yes – and it was probably the wisest decision I ever made."

The series was scheduled to start in November and two months before that Larry appeared in a tribute to Gracie Fields, the great singing star of the 1930s. The show took place in her hometown of Rochdale, at a new municipal theatre to be named after the great lady.

On the bill were Ben Warriss, Sandy Powell and the Johnny Wiltshire Orchestra – and Larry had the penultimate spot, which meant he was given the privilege of introducing Gracie, to strains of 'Sally' and a thunderous ovation. That moment was very special for Larry, who had adored 'Our Gracie' for many years and felt privileged to have got to know her in her later life.

Amazingly, after Gracie's death in 1979, he ended up owning her wedding ring. That came about because one of Larry's fans was a woman from Rochdale who had been fostered by Gracie as a child. The wedding ring had been left to her in the singer's will and she passed it on to Larry as a gift, along with a gold watch that had also belonged to Gracie's late husband, Monty Banks. Larry treasured both items which he kept in a personal jewellery case in his bedroom.

As preparations began for *The Generation Game*, it was decided that Larry should have a female assistant, to help introduce the contestants and explain the various games. A talent-spotting search went out from the BBC – and an unknown Scots folk singer by the name of Isla St Clair was selected. It was an inspired choice.

Isla and Larry clicked from day one. Off the set they became firm friends. On the screen they instantly gelled and quickly established themselves as TV's most popular double-act. One newspaper columnist called it 'an ingenious idea to pair the gloriously camp comic with a plainish girl, as thin as a stick of Edinburgh rock'.

After the opening show, Larry received a delightful letter from Arthur Marshall, a dear friend, author and himself a TV game show personality. From his home at Pound Cottage, in the Devon village of Christow, dated 4 November, 1978, Arthur wrote: 'I'm just breasting my way through the pippins (such an apple harvest we've had) to say how thrilled we all are here about your marvellous success with Generation G. You bring such charm and fun and niceness to it and everybody loves you. And nobody could be funnier! Every moment of it is an enjoyment and I am all for you taking over the entire BBC; reading the news, doing the weather forecast etc etc. Go on – I dare you! Saturday 6.45 is a lovely treat and every social invitation is refused, even early supper with my cousin Madge, in order to cluster round the box. Bless you.' Arthur signed off with: 'No answer please, your fan mail must now come by the lorry load.'

The format of the show was to pit family couples – mother or father with son or daughter – against each other in a series of weird games, to win prizes off a conveyor belt at the end. It lent itself to Larry's unscripted style, which often caused mishaps and confusion but endeared him to millions of viewers. "I made terrible mistakes but it did not matter," he reflected. "People used to say 'Did you see Larry last Saturday night when it all went wrong?' But you see, it was me being myself. After all, I had always been a mess, a living, breathing mistake."

In a radio recollection, Isla said: "Everyone responded to the warmth that Larry exuded. He gave the contestants a chance to speak and take centre stage. Spontaneous things happened but Larry was a great ad-libber and never missed the chance to lurch into something. My job was to bring people on and say wee bits and then just go along with whatever was happening and be a bit of a foil for Larry.

"On the opening rehearsal for the very first show, I was wearing a long yellow dress and as I walked down the stairs onto the set I tripped and fell my full length, landing, sprawled, at Larry's feet. His face stayed expressionless, as he simply said: 'Well, they will employ these foreigners.' It broke the ice with everybody. For the next couple of weeks after that he would look at me and remark to the backstage crew: 'She's walking better now.' Larry was so nice and kind to me. We never had a cross word and had fabulous fun. I was very proud to be part of such a successful show."

The more Larry muddled his way through – getting contestants' names mixed up, creating a rumpus demonstrating games and struggling to open jammed doors – the more the public loved it. He would get fan-mail saying such things as 'Don't worry Larry. We all make mistakes'.

The Generation Game became the most watched TV programme in the country, with weekly viewing figures rocketing over the eighteen million mark. It was recorded on the Friday and screened the following day – dominating family teatimes. Larry was amazed by its popularity. Sometimes, he would walk his dog, purposely at the same time the programme was being shown and would see his face on TV screens through the windows of house after house along the street. "I can't believe it – I'm on every single telly," he would say on his return home.

The show had many memorable, ad-libbed moments. Once, Isla was required to blow a long Swiss fugal horn. As the deep, low sound came out, Larry glanced to the audience and quipped: "She hasn't been well all day." There was also an appearance by an American marching band which caused hilarity when Larry was chided by a drill sergeant, who could barely keep a straight face as he was implored in return: "Don't forget to write."

On occasions when Larry attempted to do such things as a Morris dance or mould clay on a potter's wheel, it would all go disastrously wrong – and everyone would be in fits of laughter, including the contestants, Isla and the audience.

There were the added spin-offs, such as taking the show on tour. Larry and Isla performed scaled-down versions of *The Generation Game* at venues throughout the country, including the Civic Hall at Bedworth – a town just four miles from Nuneaton where, as a club entertainer he had performed many times. He came out with a fabulous, off-the-cuff opening line, when he looked up at a 3-D mural on the wall overlooking the stage which depicted people jiving around. "Looks like chucking out time at Mirri's," he said, referring to a pub just down the road where he would often socialise.

Larry was also invited to entertain at a children's party at Number 10 Downing Street by Labour Prime Minister James Callaghan. He was honoured to attend – even though he was a staunch Tory. On the odd occasions that politics ever entered the conversation – mainly following some item mentioned on the news – Larry always made it clear where his favours lay. He had been a long-time admirer of Winston Churchill and was a real fan of Margaret Thatcher. He once turned up at a Conservative Association garden party near Barnacle, a village just outside Nuneaton, to support an election rally hosted by Jeffrey Archer.

The Gen Game, as it became known, stayed at the top of the TV charts for four series, until, in December 1981, Larry decided to bow out. He said: "All good things must come to an end. I've enjoyed every second but I think we have done every variation of every game and the time is right to call it a day."

Larry had earned £30,000 for each show recorded during the three-year run. It had made him rich and had established him in the annals of TV folklore. Yet, for all that, his persona never changed. He refused to allow wealth or fame to go to his head. What you saw on stage or screen was what you got, at all times, with Larry. Not once did he get above his station or forget his roots. Even though he was not actually born in the town, he was proud to be known as a son of Nuneaton. He never missed an opportunity to mention his background, whether on TV in front of millions or in a private interview with a visiting journalist.

Once, he conjured up an imaginary story about Everard opening a tearoom in Chapel End. The following week a friend told Larry how he had overheard two women chatting on a bus. One said: "Did you see him on telly last Saturday? He was talking about having a café in Chapel End. I wonder where it's going to be."

After hitting the big time, Larry went one Sunday lunchtime to visit a club, in Chapel End, which was a mining district just outside Nuneaton. He walked into the bar and said: "Okay, what's everyone drinking?" To which, one of the regulars replied, in a gruff voice: "We don't want any of that big star stuff here. I'm in the chair. Now, Bill, what you havin' – a pint of mild?"

When he made the decision to finish doing *The Generation Game*, Larry received a letter from James Gilbert, head of light entertainment at the BBC. He wrote: 'I fully understand the reasons why you want to stop. Thank you for four marvellous years. It was a great achievement to follow Bruce in a highly successful series and make it not only 'your own' but an even more successful series than before.'

CHAPTER 9
ON THE MOVE TO THE
ENGLISH RIVIERA

Larry celebrated his sixtieth birthday by being the subject of a documentary, presented by Janet Street Porter. Filming took place at various locations around Nuneaton, including his home in Hinckley Road and his old Abbey Green School. Larry was surprised when he walked into Fife Street Club to be greeted by some of his former friends and neighbours, including George and Freda Smith, from the Vary Lites days. With Alec Reid on the piano, Larry serenaded the small gathering with 'In The Bushes at the Bottom of the Garden' – which he had first sung at that very same club forty-six years previously – and the programme was warmly received when it was screened at peak viewing time.

He also had a hardback book published by Macmillan with the title *Grayson's War – How Larry and his Friends Helped the War Along*. It was ghost-written and contained make-believe stories involving Larry's imaginary characters, plus poems, such as *You Can't Beat a Winkle* and recipes from the 1939 home front.

Larry now had more money in the bank than he would ever need and felt he had earned a break. Semi-retirement beckoned but he was also about to make one of the few bad decisions in his life – by leaving Nuneaton to live on the 'English Riviera'.

Before hitting the heights with *The Generation Game*, Larry had already established himself as one of the top money-earning entertainers in the country. It brought him the comfort of a nice, big house in his home town and the luxury of a chauffeur-driven Rolls Royce. In the mid-70s, he also indulged himself by buying an apartment in Torquay, to use as a holiday home for himself, Flo and family members. It was situated in a neat, modern complex, surrounded by gardens, with Cyril Fletcher, off Esther Rantzen's *That's Life TV* show, as one of his neighbours.

Larry enjoyed occasionally getting away from it all, to relax for a few days at a time on what he called 'the Beverley Hills of Torquay'. But he decided to go one step further in 1983 – by selling his Nuneaton home and upping sticks to base himself full-time in the Devon resort. It was an impulsive move, which he was later to regret.

The idea was suggested to Larry by one of his friends at the time, Barry Young, who once ran a dance school in Leicester before opening a successful hotel, Bardon Hall, just outside the city. Thoughts of having his home anywhere other than Nuneaton had never entered Larry's head. But he had been upset by a comment made during a Nuneaton and Bedworth Borough Council meeting. There had been a proposal that the local authority should consider naming something after Larry, to commemorate his rise to fame. The idea was scotched, after one Labour councillor said: "I don't think we want to be associated with someone of that ilk."

The statement was related back to Larry by a friend of his – a former mayor who was at the meeting – and he was incensed. He declared there and then to have nothing further to do with the council, once imploring me: "You had better make sure, Michael, that they don't put up any memorial to me after I've gone."

The only previous connections he had had with the

council was when he was twice invited into the civic parlour by mayors Albert Walker and Harold Jones – both times when his niece Joan visited from Canada – and when he officially opened the sheltered complex James Diskin Court in Highfield Road, Nuneaton – where his brother-in-law Charlie later went to live after May had died.

So, with the snub from the council and with Barry Young's persuasion, Larry's mind was made up: He would move to Torquay. He became convinced that a new lifestyle on the Devon coast, with its sea air and upmarket location, would be better suited for one of the country's top stars and would also be good for Flo's well-being. As it turned out, the opposite was true.

Without seeking any further advice, and without even discussing the matter with Flo or other family members, Larry made the announcement that he was leaving town. The Hinckley Road property was sold the instant it was put on the market and Larry bought an imposing house at The Lincombes in Torquay, on the side of a hill with glorious views across the bay.

Initially, he was proud of his new home. It definitely had a millionaire's setting and was certainly a far cry from Abbey Green. Although he was a totally unpretentious person, he did feel it marked an achievement, after starting out in a two-up-two-down back street terrace to ending up in a five-bedroom mansion on the sunny south coast.

Sadly, the climb to the top of the property ladder did not have a happy outcome – coinciding with, and probably conducive to, the beginning of the end for his beloved sister. After moving to Torquay, Flo was never the same person again. Her general health and, more importantly, her state of mind went rapidly downhill.

The main problem was that, despite moving to the

seaside, Larry did not have any intentions just yet of taking to his deck chair. He may have left the weekly commitment of *The Generation Game*, but he was still kept busy, fulfilling engagements throughout the country. He packed out theatres from the Isle of Wight to Sunderland, from Eastbourne to Southport. He wallowed in the opportunity to continue to play to live audiences again and meet his fans, who he never failed to disappoint as they crowded around the stage door. He was, by this time, accompanied by John Head, a northern lad who had taken over from Barry Moore as his driver and personal assistant.

So, while Larry was having the pleasure of touring and performing, it was a totally different scenario for Flo, who was left unhappily alone at the Torquay house, cut off from close contact with her family and friends and sometimes not seeing a soul for days on end. As The Lincombes was high up a steep hill, Flo's physical condition meant she could not even walk the dog or pop to the shops. Food was pre-ordered and delivered and the poor woman spent endless days on her own, simply staring out of the picture windows and padding around silent rooms, with William at her heels.

No great conversationalist anyway, Flo had never been comfortable using the phone. When he was away, Larry called her daily, just to check she was okay. That was the basic gist of the call; there was little else meaningful to chat about. It was the same if my mum or any other family member phoned. Flo would simply answer, "Yes, I'm fine. Bill will be back soon." I cannot recall a single occasion when Flo actually dialled a number and made a phone call herself.

The feeling of isolation and of being thrust into a totally alien world, eventually took its toll. Flo's mental state went into rapid decline, which, under the circumstances, was hardly surprising. It was not too long before the realisation of what was happening struck Larry and he attempted to alleviate the situation by bringing Flo back to Nuneaton whenever he was working around the Midlands. He would book the two of them into the Longshoot Motel, where they would share a room – ironically, only about a mile from where they used to live together in Hinckley Road.

One such occasion when Flo accompanied Larry was when he spent two weeks working for the Derby-based Trader Group of Newspapers. This entailed doing personal visits to a string of businesses in the ten nearby towns where the firm had a title. It was a hugely successful venture, which Larry thoroughly enjoyed.

He would be collected by a chauffeur-driven limousine, laid on by the Trader, and taken to various shops, garages, restaurants and the suchlike, where he would spend half an hour meeting staff, chatting to fans, posing for photographs and signing autographs. There would be around eight calls each day, with crowds gathering at each one. There would normally be a break for lunch, taken at a local hotel, when Larry would try to snatch a bite to eat in between again being besieged by people eager to be in the company of a famous TV star.

It was an arrangement which suited everyone. The Trader gained from selling an advertising feature on the visit; the businesses would be delighted to welcome a popular personality, which would attract customers and prestige; while Larry would earn £10,000 from ten days' work. The bonus was that he could also return to The Longshoot Motel each night to be with Flo, who had spent her day relaxing with family members and old friends.

But the change in how Flo was behaving became

worryingly and increasingly noticeable. She was more and more withdrawn, forgetful and moody, with unnatural flashes of temper. It became blatantly obvious to Larry and everyone else that something was drastically wrong. And even though clairvoyant Madame Credo had forecast that he would spend his final days in a house overlooking the sea, Larry decided to end the three-year Torquay sojourn and return to live in Nuneaton.

He asked my mum to look for a suitable place for him and Flo to live back in their hometown. Joyce spotted that in a small cul-de-sac near the town centre a pair of two-bedroom detached bungalows had just been built and were on the market. Without hesitation, Larry bought both of them and towards the end of 1986, he and Flo, accompanied by John Head, moved into Numbers 4 and 5, Harcourt Gardens.

"The original plan was that I would live in one bungalow and Flo would have the other," said Larry. "But it never worked out like that, because she was by this stage not really able to look after herself. Instead, Flo and me shared No. 4 and John occupied next door and came around to do most of our cooking. The arrangement was fine at first and, of course, when I was off working, the family were always close by to come in and help. In fact, Joyce bought a flat in the same complex, so she was just a couple of minutes away."

Larry contentedly accepted being based back on Nuneaton soil. He had a granite sign made, calling his new bungalow "Cascade" – after the name of the sanatorium-cum-rest-home in the classic Bette Davis film *Now Voyager*. Its location meant he was able to stroll most days into town, where he would stop and chat with all and sundry and shop at Marks and Spencer, his favourite store. Every Sunday morning, he would take poodle William for a walk, dropping bottles and newspapers off at the 'green' refuse banks before wandering through Riversley Park.

He looked forward to this little ritual, when he could be alone with his thoughts, as he strolled past the well-kept flower beds and beneath the drooping trees. He often made a point of looking at Flo's father's name on the stone memorial and would also be reminded of those outdoor concerts he appeared in near that very spot during the war.

Larry's career was on a wind-down, as he approached retirement age, but he agreed to host a new game show, *Sweethearts* on Anglia TV. It was promoted full of promise, as a sort of mini-*Generation Game* involving loving couples. Larry travelled every week to Norwich to record the series but it was poorly received and, by not being afforded network coverage, never took off.

He was also asked to appear in another television quiz series, *A Question of Entertainment*, recorded at the BBC Studios in Manchester. It featured Ken Dodd, Tom O'Connor and various guest stars, such as Bernard Manning, Matthew Kelly, Lionel Jeffries and Jimmy Cricket. Larry agreed to be a resident panellist and thought it would be good, light-hearted fun, centred around his love of the old movies. Instead, excerpts were shown of more up-to-date films and TV programmes, which were way outside Larry's realm of interest and whose content left a lot to be desired. He made his feelings known about the unsuitable choice of material, to no avail, and after one particularly 'crude' clip was included, he stormed off the set and quit the show.

"We were asked to identify this particular scene from a film I'd never heard about which had someone setting fire to gas coming out of a man's bottom. It was supposed to be funny but was just distasteful. That was the last straw. I refused to have anything more to do with the show," he explained.

Meanwhile, offers came in to host other TV quiz shows. He recorded a pilot for *Every Second Counts* but Paul Daniels was preferred – and the magician went on to do 142 shows over nine series. Larry was also suggested for a programme titled Beyond Belief, featuring a panel of clairvoyants, which never got past the drawing-board stage.

Performing live was Larry's real love, however, and he had a soft spot for pantomime – ever since watching his first one in Nuneaton as a four-year-old. He accepted roles in a selection of festive productions that proved there were still parts of the profession he enjoyed being involved in and also demonstrated that his popularity remained as strong as ever.

He was in *Mother Goose* at Wimbledon, alongside Honor Blackman and Dilys Watling, for a panto that received huge acclaim. He went to Leicester's De Montfort Hall in 1986 for *Snow White and the Seven Dwarfs*, leading a cast that included Ian Lavender, of *Dad's Army* fame, and Rustie Lee, a jovial Jamaican who ran a restaurant in Birmingham and had joined the growing ranks of TV chefs. Larry had a lot of fun during this show, which took record receipts.

The following Christmas he stayed local, starring at Birmingham's Alexandra Theatre, in *Dick Whittington* alongside Patrick Mower, Maggie Moone, Bernie Winters and fellow Nuneatonian Alan Randall for yet another highly-enjoyable, commercially-successful run.

In 1991 he was again tempted to venture into panto-land, to play Wishee Washee in *Aladdin* at Mansfield Civic Theatre. He obtained a part in the supporting cast for up-and-coming actor Mark Barnsley, who came from

Nuneaton and would therefore be conveniently available to drive Larry back home each night, straight after the final performance, so he could be with Flo.

By this stage, her health had become a real cause for concern and further medical tests concluded that she was suffering from dementia and Alzheimer's. Her demeanour had changed dramatically, her mind was all over the place and she was now limping worse than ever, which meant she could scarcely be left alone.

When Larry was out of the house, my mum, Joyce, would keep an eye on Flo, popping in regularly from her nearby flat to check she was okay. Even so, there were a couple of times when Flo decided to go off for a walk alone – and was found by police wandering the nearby streets, in a clearly confused and bewildered state. She told the officers she was going to see her nephew, Michael, and had got lost. At the time I was working as editor of the *Nuneaton Trader* at an office in Coton Road, which was literally two minutes away from her Harcourt Gardens bungalow but which she had been unable to find.

There was another worrying episode when Flo burned herself on a hot kettle, while trying to make a cup of tea, and she also had to receive hospital treatment when me and my mum found her nursing, and attempting to hide, a nasty dog bite on her wrist. Flo was unable to explain how it had happened, but from then on, docile poodle William had to be kept in the other bungalow whenever Larry went out.

John Head had by now departed the scene and Flo became so ill she needed round-the-clock attention. Larry was in turmoil about what to do. He considered getting in a resident nurse but in the end was forced to face the inevitable, awful, conclusion; that his dear sister needed to go into a nursing home. Despite all the guilt-ridden misgivings, he had to reluctantly accept medical advice and seek somewhere more suitable for Flo to live and be permanently looked after.

A place was soon found at Long Lea, a pleasant, privately-run establishment next to open countryside off Hinckley Road. Flo was given her own en suite room, decorated with floral wallpaper and furnished with some of her own photographs and ornaments. She was comfortably settled in and had qualified staff on hand to cater for her every need, day and night.

Larry knew he had made the right decision; that it was for her own good. But he was still, naturally, heartbroken. After all their years together, Flo had slipped, sadly and literally, into a world of her own. Her lifelong responsibility to care and worry about her little lad had come to an end. Never a woman to reveal what she was really thinking and feeling inside, the door had now firmly slammed shut.

Larry was left with a desperate feeling of emptiness. From those days tramping the clubs, from the endless tours, from the heady heights of stardom, from being feted and fan-worshipped... he had always had the comfort of knowing Flo was there, in the background, his anchor, who kept him grounded.

When all was said and done, it had only really been about just the two of them – certainly for as long as he could remember. He once told me, in one quiet reflective moment, that Flo was the only person he had ever felt deeply attached to. He said he owed her everything; that she had given up her life for him and he would never be able to repay that devotion.

During his life, as both Billy and Larry, he formed what you might call seriously close friendships with perhaps no more than a handful of people. One or two of them may have considered themselves to have been rather special to him. But, invariably, when that happened, when they got too near for comfort, when there was even the hint of something more permanent maybe developing... his barriers came up.

The question of my uncle being involved in a committed relationship with anyone – or 'saddled' as he put it – just never seemed to arise. He often used to say, casually observing a couple wandering aimlessly down the street: "Look at those two; miserable as sin, saddled with each other."

Ignoring the impulsive, short-lived dalliance with Mary Mudd, any potentially interested suitors were kept firmly at arm's length. It may have been because no one pushed the right buttons for him – or, more likely, because his heart was already taken. No other person could steal the deep-seated feelings he had for the woman who had put his welfare first. Flo's devotion was the crucial reason they were, indeed, 'saddled' – and why there was never a chance of any third party ever coming between them.

The only person to have got remotely close to doing so was Ronnie Hollis, the fey, chain-smoking pub pianist, who was Billy's almost constant companion in the late 1950s, as they frequented certain town centre pubs – renowned for attracting the more bohemian type of clientele. In public they socialised and entertained as a couple but in private their lives stayed separate.

Initially, Ronnie worked in the menswear department of JC Smith's store and there was an occasion when some new belted, gabardine raincoats had just come into stock. Ronnie immediately bought one and proudly showed it off that night when he went out for a drink. "We were propping up the bar in the Nag's Head and Ronnie was so pleased with himself, in his new, green mac," Larry recalled. "Just then a chap came through the door – wearing the exact same coat. Ronnie was livid. He took his off and threw it across a chair, while me and the rest of the gang cracked up."

When Ronnie opened a ladies hairdresser's – Roneen's, on the Cock and Bear Bridge in the sixties – Larry would call there almost daily for a cup of coffee and a chinwag. It invariably developed into a hilarious routine between the two of them, entertaining the salon customers as they sat under the dryers.

Ronnie, a slight man with a wispy, bouffant hairstyle, always addressed his friend as 'Breen'. His house in Coton Road, near the Arches, had a large billboard on the side wall with a drawing of a rampaging bull, advertising Bovril. If anyone asked where he lived, Ronnie would purse his lips and reply: "Next door to the big brown cow!"

Larry told me how he called round to Ronnie's one day to be greeted by his pal wearing a velvet smoking jacket, holding a cigarette in a long silver holder and acting strangely debonair, like a poor man's Noel Coward. "He announced that he had just had a cocktail bar installed in the front room and invited me in. As he mixed us a drink – despite it being only ten o'clock in the morning – I sat down on a low stool next to the bar. I glanced behind the soft plastic frontage – where the words 'Jaffa Oranges' could be clearly seen. The bar had been made out of some old wooden boxes from a nearby fruit shop. This was just Ronnie, a right showman and a bit of a fantasist."

There was no escaping, though, the reality of Ronnie's talents as a pianist. Self-taught, he was an absolute genius on the ivories. As well as accompanying acts on the club circuit, he would also be a sole turn at various pubs and hotels around the area. Ronnie was such a popular character that when, for example, he played at the out of the way Oddfellows Arms in Higham, he would attract a large crowd – even on a wet Wednesday night in November. Ronnie also had a dedicated following at the Griff House, between Nuneaton and Bedworth, when he would happily do requests for a large Scotch and would bring the place down with his stirring rendition of 'Rhapsody In Blue'.

Sadly, Ronnie passed away, following a short illness, before seeing 'Breen' hit the real big time. It was such a shame – I can just imagine Ronnie sitting at the piano on stage alongside Larry, on a TV set or at one of the big theatres, and being a butt of his humour. Instead of Ronnie, that role was eventually taken up by another pianist, Dennis Plowright.

Throughout his life, Larry had always enjoyed being the centre of attention and mixing with people. Whatever their personal status, whether they were single or married, male or female or – in the case of a certain songwriter – even transgender, he could greet all comers with open arms.

One of Larry's great joys was to welcome visitors into his home. From those far-off days in Clifton Road, to the more salubrious surroundings of Hinckley Road and Torquay and, eventually, to the gentile comfort of the bungalow in Harcourt Gardens, he was always the genial host.

The greeting "Come in, love, so nice to see you," would invariably be followed by an invitation to have a cup of tea – often in the company of other house callers, basking in his hospitality. A chat about news items, a recent television programme, the weather or, perhaps, the state of the country, would follow, as Larry led the conversation and kept the merriment flowing, in between doing a bit of light dusting.

On the opposite side of the coin, he also cherished moments when there was just him and Flo in the house. He used to tell me how, especially when the nights were drawing in, he loved to lock the front door, close the curtains, dim the lights, get the fire going and sit with Flo in front of the telly, before making a cup of hot cocoa and going to bed to listen to a radio play.

"I really do enjoy the simple things in life," he said. "Entertaining people is okay every now and then and I love having people round, but I'm just as happy with my own company in my own nice warm home."

Larry had lots of time for his family – the one he had been fostered into rather than the one which turned its back on him when he was born. He once confided to me that he could never forgive the fact that his real mother was made an outcast for having an illegitimate child. That's why such a link was forged between him and Flo, the woman who never questioned the origin of his existence and who would never turn her back on him.

Her reward was seeing him become comfortable and successful. Without once singing his praises or boasting of his fame, she had the satisfaction of knowing that, in her own simple, straightforward way, she had played her part. Flo cooked his meals, did his washing and ironing and sat for endless hours, waiting for him to come home safely – while he went on to have a lifestyle and career that she could never comprehend.

In showbiz circles, and sometimes during his act, Larry would refer to Flo as 'my sister Fan'. He said that was her stage name and that she had once been a great Hollywood star – in the silent movie days! He tried to bring her more into the spotlight, mentioning her name in interviews and even concocting stories about her being an ex-showgirl and how the pair of them rehearsed song-and-dance routines together at home.

It was not in Flo's nature to either get the joke or appreciate the attention. I once showed her a well-known magazine that had her photograph on the front cover, with a four-page article inside featuring 'The Woman in Larry Grayson's Life'. She hardly gave it a second glance, shrugged her shoulders and shuffled back into the kitchen. It's my guess that Flo had not learned to read and write properly. I'd certainly never seen her with a newspaper or a book in her hands and I think she could only just about sign her name. From a young age, with only a very basic education behind her, Flo had been landed with the job of looking after the family home. The only work she did all her life involved cleaning, serving, cooking or washing, so spelling and arithmetic were hardly necessary qualifications.

When the big money started to roll in for Larry, he made Flo a director of his registered company Volglade and a monthly allowance was paid into a private bank account set up in her name. I don't think she ever understood what it meant and to my knowledge, she never made any withdrawals, as Volglade looked after all the household bills. The only time I can remember her mentioning money was one lunchtime when, out of the blue, she offered to buy me a new car. I don't know what brought that about, but the subject was never mentioned again and Larry would occasionally tease her about being tight-fisted. "You know," he would say, "she won't even put her hand in her purse to pay the window cleaner!" Whatever remained in Flo's bank account was eventually swallowed up by her care home fees and she died penniless.

When it came down to it, having a well-off lifestyle did not mean a jot to Flo. Larry was more than aware of that and knew she would have been just as satisfied staying in

Clifton Road – still cooking on an old black grate and using a dolly tub to do the washing.

On the occasions when Larry hosted get-togethers for family and friends at the Hinckley Road house, Flo happily kept in the background, making sandwiches, boiling the kettle and then clearing away all the plates and glasses after the last guest had gone.

Larry appreciated her role in his life and never took Flo for granted, although she was the person on the receiving end of occasional tantrums, when some little thing or other had upset him.

There was one episode during his clubland days, when he flew into a temper because one of his stage shoes had split. As he ranted and raved, Flo did no more than put her coat on and hobble into town, using every penny she had in her handbag to buy him a new pair of patent leather shoes to wear on stage that night.

Despite being subjected to such drama-queen outbursts, Flo never once complained. The plain fact is that he could do no wrong in her eyes. If he took his frustrations out on her, she didn't bat an eyelid. He knew she was an easy target. But the woman who just as simply failed to understand his humour, also refused to be affected by his sometimes hurtful behaviour. Flo's only response was to playfully threaten to 'smack his legs'. Her prime concern was his well-being, with nothing wanted or expected in return, apart from the assurance that he was okay.

How sad, then, that Flo should be deprived of fulfilling that duty to the very end. And what a cruel conclusion of their life together for Larry, who again felt the bitter stab of abandonment. After being given away by his real mother and losing his foster mum as a young child, he was now robbed of the woman who had unconditionally filled that maternal void.

He still had family, friends and fans, who were regular visitors or were just a phone call away. Yet he couldn't help feeling empty and desolate, as he was left to soul-searchingly review his life.

It had been a search for an identity, which had been denied at birth and which had caused him so much confusion. It had been a road of discovery, of what he could achieve and what really made him tick. It had also been a quest for fulfilment, which, in the end, had been successful career-wise but a disappointing failure on a personal level.

In quiet moments he said he often wondered what would have happened if he had not been sent away as a baby to be fostered. He was raised by the family of a coal miner in the back streets of Nuneaton, yet always strangely felt drawn to his real roots, the upper middle class existence of rural Hook Norton. That old-fashioned way of life, of fields and farms and being part of a remote village community, held an in-bred appeal. His genes, his values and morals belonged more to those surroundings than the strictly down-to-earth environment he was jettisoned into.

He was forever grateful for the kindness and care shown by the Hammonds, while his affection for Nuneaton folk never wavered. And yet, there was always a niggling question-mark over the path his life had taken. Larry said to me once: "I'll never know if I was I born to turn out the way I did or whether it was because of how I was brought up. Would things have been different if I had stayed in Banbury? Would there then ever have been a Larry Grayson?"

CHAPTER 10
PERSONAL SADNESS,
FACING FINAL BOW

While he contemplated those feelings, Larry was forced to cope with being permanently parted from Flo. The decision to move her into a nursing home caused him grief and guilt. And the only way Larry could handle the distressing experience of visiting times was to switch into theatrical performance mode.

When he walked through the Long Lea doors into the lounge, where the residents sat in armchairs around the walls, it was just as if he was stepping onto a stage. He would start by making the rounds and joking with the old dears, whose eyes would fasten onto this talkative, amusing stranger. The staff would emerge from the offices or kitchens to share in the jocularity. Within minutes, Larry's appearance had literally lit up the room. That was his magic, his appeal, his unique talent. But behind the cheerful greetings, there was the hidden sadness of the real purpose of his presence – to see his beloved sister.

After the initial banter, Larry would seek out Flo, who would be curled up in a winged chair, with a woollen rug over her legs. The nursing staff, knowing of Larry's impending arrival, always washed and combed her grey wispy hair and made sure she was wearing a nice clean cardigan.

"Hello love," Larry would say, as he clutched Flo's hand. The response was a blank expression, from a woman who looked almost frightened and very old. Larry would fight away the tears and make a flippant remark to the rest of the room: "She's getting ready for her big number. Where's the tap shoes?"

Flo sat with a blank expression on her face and did not utter a single word. After a few, quiet moments together, Larry sadly whispered goodbye to Flo, who was none the wiser of who he was or what was going on.

I regularly drove him to and from these visits to Long Lea. The return journey would be in complete silence, as Larry sat in the back of the car, drained and emotional. The only consolation he had was that she was being well looked after and not in any pain or discomfort.

"The least I can do, after everything she did for me, is make sure Flo has the very best care and attention possible," he said. "It is just so upsetting to see her sitting there, not knowing where she is or who anyone is around her. When she looks at me there is no sign of any recognition. I would give up everything I have ever achieved just to hear her say once more, 'What do you fancy for tea Bill?' Flo may not remember me anymore, but I will never ever forget, or be able to repay, the debt I owe to that wonderful woman."

With just him and faithful pet poodle, William, left alone in the Harcourt Gardens bungalow – and the one next door sold to a retired couple – Larry's life slowly clicked into a lower gear. He enjoyed watching television, replaying videos from his collection of classic movies and listening to the radio.

For a short time, I lived in the bungalow next door and we would share many meal times together. He would also often pop into the Trader newspaper office, when he would entertain the staff and immediately lighten the atmosphere. There was one particular reporter, a nineteen-year-old by the name of Mark Richards, who

Larry would always tease: "Don't forget to pop round tonight. I'll leave the back door ajar," he would jokingly say to Mark, whose cheeks would immediately go bright red. It was all taken in good fun. In fact, I don't think anyone, myself included, could ever say they were not uplifted by being in my uncle's company. He had the knack of making people feel instantly happier, by just a comment or a quip.

One of his long-time acquaintances was Dagwood Hadley, who was a qualified brickie and a naturally funny man. Dag, in his trademark bobble-hat and half-hitched check trousers, did the rounds of the local pubs and clubs, accompanying a velvet-voiced singer, Norman Hussey. They were a popular duo. Their rendition of 'Every Street That You Meet is a Coronation Street' is warmly remembered and Dag's comic capers and silly jokes would complement the vocal talents of his partner, known affectionately as 'The Thrush'. Lots of people said that Dag could become a professional comedian and Larry offered to use his influence to get him some bookings. He even suggested that Dag could be a warm-up act before recordings of *The Generation Game*. Sadly, Dag suffered terribly with stage nerves. He lacked the confidence to try to make the grade – and was quite content to stay in his own backyard.

But Dag was not the least bit envious of Larry's success. In fact, he idolised my uncle. Not long before he died, Larry bumped into Dag in the town and gave him a gold lapel star, which he then wore permanently with pride and was shown off to all and sundry. As Larry's funeral cortege pulled up outside St Mary's Abbey Church, I will never forget the sight of Dag, standing at the kerbside holding his tartan hat to his chest, with tears streaming down his face.

Larry's career perked up after he made an appearance on a *This Is Your Life* tribute to one of his old showbiz friends Jill Summer, the *Coronation Street* actress. It prompted a stream of offers of work, including being a guest on Michael Aspel's top-rated chat show, doing a summer season in Torquay and returning to panto in Wimbledon.

The bookings were gratefully accepted but Larry had started to become somewhat disillusioned by the business. The public acceptance and appreciation of his camp style had opened the TV doors for such people as Julian Clary, Graham Norton and Paul O'Grady. But Larry couldn't abide the new fad for 'in your face' humour. He preferred subtlety to smut, class to crassness.

His political persuasion and his affections for royalty may have had a blueish tinge – but Larry had no time at all for off-colour language. He used to joke: "If someone starts getting undressed on TV or uses swear words, I have to cover my dog's eyes and ears."

Against his better judgement, Larry agreed to go on a late night talk show on London Weekend Television. "It was live and I knew straightaway, from the opening comments from the other guests, that I did not belong there," he said. "The business was no longer what I was used to. The producer was only twenty-three and there was no respect. I had been brought up with real professional theatre people, who had polish and discipline with no time for offensive material. This programme went against all those ideals. In the car afterwards, on the way home, my manager looked at my face and said: 'You're not doing any more are you?' I said, 'No, that's the finish.'"

One thing which perturbed Larry was the way that performers such as Clary and Norton so openly portrayed their sexuality. He told me he was offended if people described him as a gay entertainer, although he had no problems with the 'camp' label, which was more affectionately attached. He was happy to consider his act 'camp' alongside the definition of it being slightly frivolous and quaintly effeminate. Sometimes he would joke that people thought it was a reference to him entertaining at holiday camps – which, in fact, he never did.

Larry was particularly annoyed when he was approached by members of the Gay Rights Movement, who wanted him to carry their banner. "Under no circumstances," he replied. He always held the belief that people's sexual orientation and preferences were things to be kept private, behind closed doors. He never, openly, admitted being homosexual and never left himself liable to accusations of untoward behaviour.

He was born a Virgo – and, to all intents and purposes, and certainly to the outside world, remained one. When he became famous, Larry said to me: "The papers will be trying their hardest to find some dirt about me. But there's nothing. I've never stepped out of line." Indeed, not one scurrilous article, not one damaging headline, not one sniff of scandal ever appeared against his name – even after his death. If anything, he was the darling of the media, who wrote and said nothing but nice things about him.

Manager Paul Vaughan, who looked after his business affairs for over twenty years, said: "I sincerely believe Larry was asexual. He just wasn't interested in that sort of thing. If sex was ever on his agenda at all, it was certainly never very high. He was not interested in gay clubs or the gay scene or anything like that. He would much rather be having a drink at the Chapel End Miners Welfare Club where he was liked and where the blokes would simply say: 'You all right, mate?' That was a much nicer environment to him. You see, Larry had been brought up without any great male influence in his life where everything in his younger days was domestic and warm. He endeared himself to a large proportion of his audience who were made up of ladies of a certain age. They were blue rinsed and they adored him."

Paul had taken over the management reins while Larry was doing *The Generation Game*. Although he was still officially on the books of Peter Dulay, Larry had become unhappy with some of the financial arrangements that had been made on his behalf. He was especially perturbed by an allegation, made to him by a well-wisher, that some royalties from a record deal had been misappropriated.

Queries had also been raised by Larry's bank manager at the time and he took it on himself to make contact with Paul Vaughan, a show business agent who hailed from Birmingham. The upshot was that Paul was introduced to Larry, who then invited him to become his manager. "Peter Dulay still had the rights to claim for the *Gen Game* work, but Larry let it be known that I was now authorised to deal with anything further," said Paul. "We went on to have a very happy business relationship and it is something I will always cherish."

As he gradually slipped into retirement, Larry looked back on a fifty-year showbiz career with fondness. "To go on stage and make people laugh is just marvellous. When you walk out and hear the applause it is the most rewarding thing in the world. I was fortunate to be born with a wonderful sense of humour. I could laugh at the least thing, including myself. I was given a gift to make people laugh and I thank God for that."

He did a *Late Night with Larry* radio show on the BBC, when he talked about his career and played selections of his favourite music, which included more than a smattering of songs from films. He was a devout fan of the big MGM musicals and, obviously, never missed an opportunity to include selections from Judy Garland.

He also appeared on a radio breakfast show with local lad, Jim Lee, at BBC's Coventry studios. I offered to drive him there – and it was one of those days when Larry was in absolutely dazzling form. He took phone calls from fans and people who knew him in the Billy Breen era. His guest spot should have been for twenty minutes – instead, Larry stayed on air for the whole two hours, chatting away about the old times and recalling the names of individual pianists and entertainment secretaries from years gone by.

As a dedicated Anglophile, going abroad on holidays never held much appeal for him. The only travelling he really enjoyed was when he went 'on the road' for appearances at theatres, TV studios or charity functions. Larry turned down an offer to visit Australia in the late seventies but he did venture as far as Hollywood, when he stayed with a friend and met the daughter of comedy hero Stan Laurel. The highlight of this trip was to see and feel the handprints of Judy Garland, placed in concrete on the famous 'Walk of Fame' outside Grauman's Chinese Theatre.

Approaching his seventieth birthday, Larry made two other journeys overseas. He spent a week in sweltering heat in Tunisia, when he hardly left his hotel room, and was then talked into experiencing completely different weather conditions on a post-Christmas trip to Austria. This was a far from merry occasion, because Larry slipped on ice on New Year's Eve and broke several ribs.

He saw in 1993 from a hospital bed in Saltzburg and was eventually flown back to Coventry Airport by a chartered ambulance plane to spend a few days in Nuneaton's Manor Hospital before being allowed home. "That was no fun at all – and that's the last time I'll ever go away on holiday," he said.

The rib injury was followed by further health problems. Larry went into a private hospital at Hill Top, Nuneaton, for operations on varicose veins and glaucoma, before his old ulcer troubles reappeared.

He celebrated his seventy-first birthday quietly at Harcourt Gardens and then made a surprise, unpublicised return to the TV screen, organised through a phone call from a friend from years ago, Kevin Bishop, who was now a top producer tasked with staging the *1994 Royal Command Performance*. He told Larry that lots of people had been asking after him and it would be a great idea to make a guest appearance. Without bothering to consult his manager Paul Vaughan, Larry accepted the invitation.

His five-minute cameo spot at the Dominion Theatre, in the presence of Prince Charles, turned out to be Larry's TV farewell. He walked out, carrying his gold-painted bentwood chair, as the orchestra played 'The Man That Got Away'. His opening line: "My legs are giving me hell," was followed by: "I only came here so you can see I'm still alive. But I'm all right. I can walk without a frame. I still have my own hair and my face has not been lifted." Larry bowed out with the words: "To all the people at home, I must just say it once, 'Shut That Door'. I love you all."

Larry delighted in the applause and reception he received. But he looked tired and drawn, which was not helped by persistent pains in his stomach. As someone who always held doctors in awe, Larry refrained from seeking medical attention, instead relying on his usual remedy of nicotine and gin. Over the years, whenever he suddenly resorted to smoking cigarettes and drinking large G&Ts, it was invariably a signal that he was having tummy-trouble. This was again the case in the days following his Royal

Command appearance. My mum expressed concern but Larry just shrugged it off as he prepared for a quiet Christmas at home.

In an interview with Margaret Forwood in the *Daily Express*, published on 27 December, 1994, he was quoted as saying: "I don't feel old. It's an attitude of mind. I'm lucky, I've got a marvellous memory. I remember everyone I've ever met, every theatrical landlady I ever stayed with. I make myself laugh, remembering things I said or should have said. I fall about laughing. I've had a wonderful life. I've been lucky. It'll make a marvellous film when I'm gone."

Five days later, on 1 January, Larry was found collapsed in agony in his bungalow by next-door neighbours Joan and Ken Harris. They called my mum, Joyce, from her flat at the end of the close, who dialled 999 for an ambulance. Larry was admitted into George Eliot Hospital, Nuneaton, for an operation on a perforated appendix.

Larry overcame surgery and recovered well enough to receive visitors and keep the staff amused. As it happened, I was also in the hospital at the same time, due to a bit of a heart issue. I was on Dolly Winthrop Ward and Larry was next door on Bob Jakin. "Dolly Winthrop and Bob Jakin – sounds like a music hall double act," he quipped.

I was discharged on 6 January and called in to see my uncle on my way out of hospital. He was sitting up in his side room, surrounded by 'Get Well' cards and seemed fine. He made a joke about two bed pans that had been put side-by-side on a nearby table 'like a pair of shoes'. As I prepared to leave, he said: "Off you go then. I'll be home tomorrow – see you at the bungalow."

Unbeknown to me or any of the family, a short while later the doctors decided that Larry was okay to leave that night. A call was made to old friends Barry Anthony and

Ray Young, who had travelled down from their home in Barnsley specially to look after him and were stopping at his bungalow. They fetched him from the hospital and he arrived back at Harcourt Gardens at 6.15 p.m. Just six hours later Larry was dead, suffering a massive internal haemorrhage while lying in his own bed.

Barry said: "He had settled down and seemed quite comfortable. Around midnight, I popped in to see if he was okay or wanted anything. He was awake and I tried to lighten things up by telling him how fabulous his skin looked. I said it looked better than mine, even after all the money I'd spent on face products. He replied: 'And you think we don't know?' Then he suddenly sat bolt upright, looked straight past me, went 'Ooh' and fell back, unconscious. I couldn't believe it. In an instant, he was gone."

A distraught Barry phoned my mum. She ran from her nearby flat to the bungalow but realised it was too late. An ambulance arrived, followed by a doctor, who confirmed Larry's death. Mum phoned me straightaway and arrived at my house with Barry to fetch me back to the bungalow. The next few hours were spent in a state of numbed shock. We sat there, with the curtains drawn, as the news that 'Larry Grayson, the star of *The Generation Game* had died suddenly today' was relayed to the nation on the 7.00 a.m. TV and radio bulletins. It felt quite unreal, the way his face kept appearing on the screen, accompanying the awful announcement. I found it very difficult to accept that I would never again see my uncle Bill, especially after having a laugh with him in hospital just the day before.

Manager Paul Vaughan soon turned up from his home in Worcester and took charge of making the press announcements and fending off a stream of callers to the front door. A posse of photographers and reporters had already gathered at the end of the drive, trying to gather more details about the tragedy of a man who had brought so much joy into so many lives.

Larry's *Generation Game* partner, Isla St Clair, was given the news in a phone call at 8.20 a.m. She said: "A cameraman who had worked with us rang me and said he was sorry to hear about Larry. I thought he was referring to his operation and I said, 'Oh, he is doing fine. In fact, he might be back home now.' He then said, 'No, Isla. Larry's dead.' I could not believe it. I was planning to call Larry that very day to wish him happy New Year. I was absolutely stunned. I have many wonderful memories of such a sweet man, who gave so much pleasure to so many people, of all walks of life."

The following day, newspapers throughout the country carried front page reports. One headline called it 'A Gray Day as Top Comic is Mourned'. Another read: 'The Loner Who Just Wanted to be Loved'. Tributes were paid by many showbiz stars, including fellow comedians.

Bernard Manning said: "He was in the top ten in the world. All he needed to do was give a look, fold his arms and say 'Shut that door'. He will be sadly missed."

Bob Monkhouse said: "No matter how close to the wind he sometimes sailed, his sweetness of nature and obvious best intentions prevented him from giving offence."

Ken Dodd said: "His timing was impeccable and he had a wonderful face, which showed his trials and tribulations and which is good for an audience to warm to. He was a very brilliant man."

Actress June Whitfield said: "He was unique. He brought a great response from an audience and was a delightful chap."

Actor Richard Briers said: "Larry's appeal really did cross the generation gap."

The official cause of death, determined by a post mortem, was 'upper gastro-intestinal bleeding due to a duodenal ulcer'. It was deemed 'natural causes', unconnected with his operation, although both me and my mum felt that questions should have been asked about the circumstances of Larry's discharge from hospital on the night he died.

Flags flew at half-mast throughout Nuneaton – including one on the pole outside his former home in Hinckley Road. In his will, Larry left family bequests and gifts and also stipulated that at his funeral, instead of floral tributes, donations should be made to the George Eliot Hospital Scanner Appeal, of which he was a patron. He had lent his name to that appeal right from its launch in 1993 when he delivered a stirring, off-the-cuff speech in front of doctors, staff, patients and civic dignitaries in the hospital canteen.

Over the years, Larry made many personal appearances to help local charities and voluntary groups. He was guest of honour at the 1979 opening of the Riding for the Disabled Centre at Galley Common – when he was enticed into posing for a photograph on horseback – while he also willingly supported the town's Mary Ann Evans Hospice. He felt highly honoured to be asked to officially start the traditional Atherstone Ball Game – staying right to the end to join in the celebrations at The Angel pub with the winning team – and was always happy to turn out at garden fetes and carnivals. One unusual function attracted lots of publicity for a small village, Norton-Juxta-Twycross, near Atherstone, when Larry officially opened the community centre's new toilets!

The grief of his sudden death was felt by family members, friends, colleagues, associates and legions of fans throughout the country. One person was still unaware, however, and it was left to me and my mum to take on the unpleasant, daunting task of breaking the news to Flo, who remained totally oblivious in Long Lea nursing home.

She was by now very ill and had slipped into a comatose-like condition. A staff member told us that Flo had been confined to bed, without opening her eyes or uttering a sound, for some time. Despite this, mum felt that Flo needed to be told what had happened, even if she was past the stage of being able to understand.

We went into her room quietly. The curtains were drawn and there was a pink glow from a small lamp. We sat down on either side of the bed. Flo was lying motionless on her back, with her arms outside the sheets, on top of a quilted bedspread. Her face, framed with strands of grey hair, looked tiny on the large white pillow. Mum took hold of one of her hands and whispered into her ear that she was sorry to say that Billy had passed away.

I saw Flo squeeze my mum's hand ever so gently, as a single tear trickled down her cheek and dripped onto her chin. It was heart-rending. She must have known what was said but there was no further reaction. Flo's frail fingers slowly fell limp and her eyelids remained closed. We stood in silence for a few minutes before giving my dear aunty a kiss and leaving her in peace.

Larry's funeral took place on 16 January, at St Mary's Abbey Church, literally round the corner from Stanley Crescent, where William Sully White had first arrived as a babe in arms.

The hearse left Harcourt Gardens and, on its way, stopped briefly at Abbey Green in front of the site of young Billy's first-ever stage, behind what was once a row of terraced cottages and was now a council car park.

The Rev Robert Marshall and Canon John Graty conducted the service at the Abbey Church, where every seat inside the ancient building was taken. There was a loudspeaker link to people massed outside on a cold, but clear morning. It looked as if almost the whole of Nuneaton had turned out to pay their respects to the town's most famous and favourite resident. As we made our way into the church I spotted many familiar faces, including old neighbours from Clifton Road and people my uncle had known and befriended over the years.

Among the mourners from the entertainment world were *Crossroads* actress Jane Rossington, *Coronation Street*'s Johnny Briggs, BBC chat show hostess Judy Spiers, television producer Alan Boyd and a tearful Isla St Clair.

The service began with an organist playing a medley from *The Wizard of Oz*, before the church choir sang three Funeral Sentences. Following a bidding prayer and the hymn, *Praise My Soul the King of Heaven*, I stepped forward to recite a passage from The Book of Revelation IV, 1-8. The opening words were: 'After this I looked and, lo, in heaven an open door'. The second verse contained the phrase: 'Round the throne was a rainbow that looked like an emerald...'

The second lesson – from Mark IX, 2-8 – was read by showbiz friend Dora Bryan, who had travelled up that morning from Brighton and had joined us for a cup of tea in Harcourt Gardens before setting off for the church. She told the congregation: "Larry gave us all wonderful laughter and wonderful memories."

An address was given by the Rev Marshall, the actors' union priest and Bishop of London press secretary who had first got to know Larry when he interviewed him eighteen years previously. He said: "He brought happiness and fun to millions of people's lives. He broke down the barriers and made people laugh at themselves and look at the bright side of life."

The order of service contained a quote from Joyce Grenfell: '*If I should go before the rest of you, break not a flower*

121

nor inscribe a stone, nor when I'm gone speak in a Sunday voice, but be the usual selves that I have known. Weep if you must; parting is hell. But life goes on, so laugh as well'. There was also a revised verse from a Judy Garland song: *'Now the time has come for breaking up the party, and the curtain up above us has to fall. I don't want to be a bore, but it's time to Shut That Door...that's all, that's all.'*

Hymns *The Lord's My Shepherd, How Great Thou Art* and *Jerusalem* were sung and a blessing was read as the coffin was carried from the church. At a reception at The Chase Hotel – where Flo had once worked as a cleaner when it was a private house – a string quartet played a selection of Judy Garland songs.

After a private cremation, Larry's ashes were buried in the family grave at Oaston Road cemetery – alongside the remains of his real mum, Ethel, and the couple who agreed to foster him, Jim and Alice Hammonds.

A charity concert, in Larry's name, took place at Bedworth Civic Hall on 3 May. The cast included Isla St Clair and Barry Anthony and Ray Young, and raised £2,000, to add to the £3,246 collected from funeral donations in aid of the George Eliot Hospital Scanner Appeal.

Two months later a memorial service was organised at the 'Actors' Church, St Paul's in Covent Garden, London – near the theatre where Larry had watched Judy Garland in concert and not far from his own triumph at The Palladium. It was attended by scores of showbiz colleagues and acquaintances, including Danny La Rue, Rod Hull, The Beverley Sisters, Mollie Sugden, Lionel Blair, Judy Spiers, Cliff Michelmore and Gretchen Franklin. Many people from Nuneaton also made the journey to join the congregation, including friends and relatives, the mayor Don Jacques and the town's MP, Bill Olner.

Touching tributes were paid by Terry Wogan and Roy Hudd. Terry said: "Larry Grayson had an eye like a hawk. He once spotted dandruff on me and stopped me in mid-sentence to declare: 'Your hair needs washing.' It was a privilege and a pleasure to have your frail ego slashed to ribbons by a professional like Larry. No comedian, with the possible exception of Jack Benny, took more risks. He would walk on stage and fix them with that stare and wait, and wait, and wait, until they cracked. I just wish he was here now. He would complain about the dust in this church, rearrange the flowers, criticise my weight and just flounce off. There will never be another like him."

In his homage, Roy Hudd said: "You could not see the join between Larry on and off stage. Of all the comedians I have known, he made me laugh as much off stage as on it. He was unique, every bit a pro and I loved him for it."

The acclaim was richly deserved for someone who had made such a telling mark on his profession. Publicly, he had achieved his ambition, of being a star and receiving nationwide adoration. But privately, this gentle man with a mixed-up background never attained the same heights of fulfilment. As he wallowed in the applause at the end of his shows he may have mouthed the words: "I love you all." But his heart really only belonged to one person – a very special lady who most definitely was his No. 1 fan.

'I CAN ONLY GIVE YOU LOVE THAT LASTS FOREVER AND A PROMISE TO BE NEAR EACH TIME YOU CALL. AND THE ONLY HEART I OWN IS FOR YOU AND YOU ALONE, THAT'S ALL.'
~ Judy Garland song

EPILOGUE

Flo remained impassively in her room at Long Lea for another twelve months after Larry's death and then passed away – as she had lived her life, with the minimum of fuss – on 27 January, 1996, aged eighty-seven. Me and my mum watched her take her last breath, after being summoned by nursing home staff in an early morning phone call. Flo's funeral took place at Nuneaton's Heart of England Crematorium and her ashes were placed in the grave at Oaston Road, next to those of the boy who had been the centre of her whole life. It was the final act of reunion of two people who had shared an incredible journey from lowly beginnings to the peak of national adulation.

After leaving Abbey Green, living in Priory Street and being bombed out of Harefield Road, Flo and Billy moved with their dad, Jim Hammonds, into 52 Clifton Road, which was then their home for nearly thirty years. The house initially had no bathroom and the loo was outside, in the yard. The cooking was done on an open fire in a back kitchen, reached via the front parlour or through the back door, off an entry. Upstairs was tiny. Flo always had the front bedroom, while Billy and Jim slept in the other room, across the one-step landing. Looking back, it's quite amazing to realise that when Billy was on the brink of becoming the nation's No. 1 entertainer, he was in his late forties and still did not have his own bedroom, sleeping in a twin bed alongside an elderly ex-miner.

Even so, he and Flo had many happy memories of Clifton Road. When the old black grate was removed and when a modern ground-floor bathroom was added on the back, they thought things were really looking up.

The main living area was the kitchen, which also contained a dining table and settee. Jim had his chair and sat there puffing away on a pipe. Flo would be almost permanently standing, propped against the sink or the cooker. Billy would be flicking around with a feather duster or welcoming an almost endless stream of visitors, calling in for a chinwag or to use the street's only phone. He would hear the local gossip, listen to tales of woe, giggle at their idiosyncrasies and make mental notes to store away for future use.

Much of the content of his stage act originated in Clifton Road, with Flo a blissfully unaware bystander. While Billy went to work, slogging his way around the local clubs and provincial theatres, her main occupation was to look after the home and make sure the kettle was always on.

As a housekeeper, Flo performed wonders. She made every penny count from whatever little she or Billy earned and there was no shortage of hearty, fresh meals. She scrimped and saved enough to buy little 'luxury' items, such as tins of salmon and peaches, which would be stored away for special occasions, such as Sunday afternoon teas served in the front parlour – where the 22-inch telly stood, next to Billy's polished wood gramophone.

Flo did all the clothes washing by hand; there was simply no room for a machine. She would carry the shopping home from town – and woe betide her if she forgot to bring any pork dripping from Bostocks!

So that was life at Clifton Road, a place which often echoed with the howls of laughter but where there were also tears of sadness, brought about by the deaths of Jim and Ethel and the serious illness of Billy. It was also the springboard for England's newest comedy sensation –

when Flo's world turned upside down.

The move to the detached house at 85 Hinckley Road – in one of Nuneaton's up-market areas – was greeted with delight by the family. Flo was a little bewildered by having so much extra room – including a large garden and vegetable plot. She never quite came to terms with having the help of a cleaner but gradually began to accept and even enjoy her new, spacious surroundings. The arrival of sister May and her husband Charlie, to live in a house over the road, was a bonus for Flo, while she also had the treat of being taken to have her hair done in a chauffeur-driven Rolls Royce.

There was a large garden – looked after by a friendly next-door neighbour – where ageing poodle, Peter, could romp to his heart's content, among the rows of cabbages and bean plants, while family get-togethers became an even more regular occurrence in the newly-installed bar, complete with optics and green padded high stools.

For Flo, it was like a mansion compared to anything she had known before and she soon began to feel at home, occasionally indulging in a tipple of sherry – usually as she waited in the early hours for the man of the house to return.

It was when the scenario switched to Torquay that Flo suffered. Being uprooted from Nuneaton and being subjected to endless days of isolation – at such a crucial age – set her on a downward spiral. The shame was that by the time, three years later, Flo had come back to live in her home town, the damage had been done. Sadly, she was never able to fully appreciate the pleasantness of her cosier surroundings in Harcourt Gardens, as the onset of dementia quickly took its toll.

It was especially poignant that Flo should end her days in a nursing home, among complete strangers, apart from the person who had meant everything in the world to her and whose presence had become so tragically wiped from her memory.

She never had any desire for personal possessions or pleasures; her sole purpose was to care about the welfare of a boy who came out of nowhere and then embarked on a journey to the stars. Flo was with him through it all, from that makeshift backyard stage to the glamorous heights of the most hallowed theatre in the land and onto the TV screens of millions of people. But she was content to stay in the wings, while he took the applause. Many doors were opened for both of them along the way before the final curtain came down.

Billy took his bow first, without warning, to cause shock and create news headlines, Flo made her exit twelve months later, without a whimper after having her memories frozen inside an already locked mind.

As a couple, their personalities were at opposite ends of the spectrum. Biologically, they may or may not have been related. But no bond, through blood or contact, could ever have been stronger.

Billy and Flo – joined forever by fate and separated by illness – were reunited in death, with their caskets lying next to one another in a tree-shrouded burial plot and their names engraved in gold on the same black marble headstone.

'EVER SINCE THE WORLD BEGAN THERE IS NOTHING SADDER THAN... THE ONE MAN WOMAN LOOKING FOR THE MAN THAT GOT AWAY'.
~ Judy Garland song

POSTSCRIPT

An exhibition, looking back at Larry Grayson's life and career was staged at the Museum and Art Gallery in Nuneaton's Riversley Park in July 1999. It stayed on the upstairs gallery for three months and was featured on regional television and in national newspapers.

Nine years later, a permanent tribute to the town's most famous son was installed in the ground floor local history gallery and many of Larry's personal artefacts and trophies were put on display, including his Palladium dressing room door plaque and the bow tie he wore when he was presented to the Queen.

In May, 2006, the British Comedy Society unveiled a plaque in honour of Larry at the Shepherd's Bush Empire – where *The Generation Game* used to be recorded. The blue plate was placed in the foyer at a ceremony attended by, among others, Sir Terry Wogan, Sir Billy Cotton, Sir Norman Wisdom, Dame Dora Bryan and Billy Tallon, who had been on the Queen Mother's staff and who had once secretly invited Larry back to St James's Palace for a cup of tea.

Following the plaque unveiling, a celebration lunch was held at the nearby Kensington Hilton Hotel, where Paul Vaughan and Isla St Clair paid tributes. Paul said: "It would have gladdened Larry's heart to know he was being remembered and honoured by such a richly diverse company." Isla said: "Larry had a wonderful way of making everyone he came into contact with feel like a special friend."

Meanwhile, official recognition in Larry's hometown

remained largely noticeable by its absence. A half-hearted proposal a few years ago to install a memorial as part of a facelift to Abbey Green came to nothing, while suggestions for the council to erect a plaque or title a street or building after the star also received little support, although a refurbished town centre pub was unveiled in May, 2010 as The William White, after one of his childhood names.

But the last laugh goes to Larry. Once, when someone mentioned to him that there should be a statue to him in Nuneaton, he quickly replied: "There already is." To the woman's amazement, Larry said: "You know the statue in Newdegate Square depicting George Eliot? Well, that's really me in that bonnet and shawl. I was the model for it – but don't tell anyone."

ABOUT THE AUTHOR

Mike Malyon is a great nephew of William Sully White, better known as 1970s' comedian and TV presenter, Larry Grayson.

Mike first saw his uncle performing on stage around the local clubs under the name of Billy Breen. Mike then followed and shared the camp comic's dramatic rise to stardom, when Larry topped the bill at the London Palladium, headlined sell-out shows throughout the UK, appeared on This Is Your Life and eventually hosted the chart-topping TV programme The Generation Game.

Larry was adored by millions but the person who knew him best was his foster sister, friend and companion, Flo. Mike was close to both his uncle and aunt and inherited all their personal photographs, scrapbooks and memorabilia. He has also taken on the role of preserving the memory of a man whose ambition, from an early age, was to be an entertainer and who spent his life desperately seeking attention.

Mike is a retired journalist who lives in the Nuneaton area.

www.apexpublishing.co.uk

CPSIA information can be obtained
at www.ICGtesting.com
Printed in the USA
BVHW030913170220
572559BV00001B/63